Leadership Skills Reduce The Bills

6 Steps Every Leader Must Know To Reduce
Staff Turnover and Increase Productivity

Lisa Wiking

GOWOR
INTERNATIONAL PUBLISHING

Leadership Skills Reduce the Bills: 6 Steps Every Leader Must Know to Reduce Staff Turnover And Increase Productivity Lisa Wiking 2015

www.motivationalleadership.com.au

The moral rights of Lisa Wiking to be identified as the author of this work have been asserted in accordance with the Copyright Act 1968.

First published in Australia 2015 by Gowor International Publishing.

www.goworinternationalpublishing.com

ISBN 978-0-9925258-7-3

Any opinions expressed in this work are exclusively those of the author and are not necessarily the views held or endorsed by Gowor International Publishing.

Disclaimer

Dedicated to...

My Parents, Mary and Anders Wiking, for
believing in me and guiding me.

Alison Crabb, for always believing in me and giving me
the opportunity to be a leader all those years ago.

All members of all of my teams, thanks for the fun and good times.

My partner Darren, for your support and continuing belief in me.

For my daughter Kiara and unborn son, I hope you
can take the lessons in this book and apply them in
your life and career, whatever you choose to do.

A Personal Note from the Publisher

Hi there!

As the Founder of Gowor International Publishing, my publishing house, I make it part of my practice to offer a personal review for the authors of books we publish, which they can share with others. I do this so that you, the reader, can glean a further understanding into why this book is about to become a valuable part of your life.

Having said this, let me tell you about Lisa and why this book will benefit you. There is no doubt that to be a leader requires certain qualities from within us. It requires strength to endure difficult circumstances and people's opinions. It requires heart to lead people so they know that you care. And it requires ambition, which gives rise to vision and, ideally, accomplishment. Lisa has all of these qualities within her. Having known Lisa for several months now, I believe that she is a true leader. She is one of the strongest women I know, both personally and professionally, and what I love even more than her self-evident strength is her deep connection to the heart of leadership. I know that she is a true leader. She is also one of the most sensitive women I know, and that is heart-touching. I have been continually moved by watching how Lisa tackles her goals and aspirations in life, including the creation of this book and the brilliant body of work that exists within it. Lisa stops at nothing when it comes to providing a service that she can be proud of and that will make a significant impact in the lives of others.

She has courage and she isn't afraid of the hard work required to build a legacy - one which she is fast creating. This book, *Leadership Skills Reduce the Bills*, is a reflection of everything that Lisa is. It is a guide that has the power to help you rise up in leadership, obtain a position of leadership, or improve your current expression of leadership in your job, business and life. It is grounded in Lisa's extensive and impressive experience in the field, and packed with knowledge that you can take and apply right here, right now, in order to make a difference in the lives of those around you. It will teach you how to lead from the front and take your team and the people you care for to great places.

It has been a deep honour to work with Lisa as this book has come to life and I know that, like me, you will love it. Enjoy the book.

Emily Gowor
Founder of Gowor International Publishing

Contents

PART 6: Game Plan

Foreword

by Alison Crabb

I first met Lisa Wiking as a bright-eyed, bushy-tailed young lady back in the mid-90's, when she joined my business as a novice travel consultant. It was clear to me she was someone full of passion and enthusiasm, and naively wanted to change the world to make a difference for others. From the moment I met her, I knew that she would grow to be a successful leader. She was what I would call a "natural born leader." She demonstrated all of the qualities that you would want to see in a leader. For example, she was always open to feedback, always asking questions with a willingness to learn, and she was someone who was willing to take ownership and responsibility for both the good and bad. Lisa was very much a "feel the fear and do it anyway" kind of person.

Very early in her career and with very little experience, she was given her first taste of leadership. Her first challenge was a big one. I gave her one of our most underperforming businesses, which needed a new team and a huge rebuild, including having to recruit new staff and train them.

She set about creating a vision and goal for the business, with some very simple strategies to improve sales and improve the customer experience. She worked incredibly hard, developed a great staff, and within 18 months, the business was flourishing. Results improved with a turnaround of almost $150,000, and the business was one of the most improved businesses in Victoria that year. The following year, we saw even better results: she had grown the profit by a further 20%.

For 20 years, I have watched her journey from that young lady to a wonderful leader and businesswoman, passionate about leadership and dedicated to helping businesses improve their results.

In 1999, I took a sabbatical from the business to take on the role of motherhood, and a few years later Lisa also left to pursue her life passion – executive coaching. A few years later, I returned to the business and, on occasion, would contact Lisa to see how she was and would quietly sound her out about coming back.

It wasn't until late 2010 that I was in need of a leadership coach and trainer to work with our newer leaders. We had just grown our business dramatically in a very short period, and needed experience fast. I knew the perfect person for the job.

This time I was very excited that she said yes!

After a short period of time, an area leader position became available, and she applied for it, as this was, as Lisa would call it, her "dream job".

As she developed as an area leader, she did a wonderful job showing all of those amazing qualities I had seen in her so many years ago, this time leading over 100 people in her team.

She had grown and matured as a leader, used all of her coaching knowledge and skill, and did a fantastic job of developing great culture and community amongst the team.

I have a watched Lisa impact the lives of many and be a role model to people who have gone on to be very successful leaders themselves. Sometimes, running a business can seem overwhelming, with so many parts of the business to juggle. Many small businesses do not have the resources – such as recruitment teams, large sales teams and marketing teams – and are often in need of guidance and business ideas to help them improve. Large corporate companies who have plenty of resources often have difficulty developing and implementing business systems and managing their staff effectively.

All of the strategies in this book come from Lisa's personal knowledge and experience of leading small teams and multiple businesses at the same time. The information contained within is certainly a solution to many of the challenges highlighted above.

Running the most successful business is not always smooth sailing, and Lisa highlights some of her greatest mistakes and lessons learnt along the way as well.

I highly recommend this book to anyone who is seeking step-by-step strategies to improve their results and wants to make the job of leading a business simpler.

Preface

This book is a compilation of all that I have learned around leadership and what I believe is required to be a successful leader. As I have shared with many leaders I have worked with, you must start with the end in mind, so it would be remiss of me to write a book without doing the same.

The content in this book is by no means the only way to be a successful leader, but for those who haven't yet experienced the privilege of leadership, it can be a daunting experience. My intention is to simply help you overcome any fears and give you the information that I would have loved when I first stepped up in 1999. For readers who are currently in a leadership position, my intention is to share with you a new way which, if you apply it, will help you simplify not only your role as a leader, but also your life, if you choose.

Like the coach of any professional sports team will say when the team loses a match, "It's about regaining focus and getting it back to basics." This book is all about the basics of leadership. If you understand what is important and you do it well, then you will have great success as a leader.

In order to give you some framework, I'll share with you a little about my story, so you can see that if I can do it, then anyone can.

I started working with Flight Centre Ltd on the 28th August, 1997, and yes, I was 12 years old. No, not really, but I was a youngster. I was 20 years of age and I hadn't travelled by myself, had no sales experience and failed the first year of university, so I didn't meet any of the requirements for obtaining a job with Flight Centre. Having worked as a receptionist and a gaming cashier on the graveyard shift, I saw this as the opportunity of a lifetime. I wanted this job so badly I even bought a bright red jacket so that I would stand out in the group interview.

Surprisingly, I was successful in the interview and I was offered a position at *Great Holiday Escape Eastland*, my local shopping centre in the Eastern Suburbs of Melbourne, Australia. At that time, we did three weeks of training in order to learn the ropes of becoming a travel agent. We would spend half our day training in the back office and half our day serving "real" customers out the front.

I felt like I was in a foreign land with no idea how to speak the language. I have often shared with my team members when they first begin, that I struggled to string a sentence together for the first three months. Learning to become a travel agent is more complicated than what it first appears, keeping in mind that our product is the world and there are a million different systems to learn. Sometimes it feels like you're expected to know everything on day one. Sharing this validated my new team members and made it okay for them to feel a little nervous, too.

As time passed and what felt like "the most difficult job in the world" was getting easier and easier, however I still wasn't enjoying it as much as I thought I would. I knew it had something to do with the leader of the business, because the atmosphere of the workplace wasn't positive or successful.

There were many days when I didn't feel that I was welcome in the team or valued as a team member. I went home most nights crying, saying to friends and family that I didn't know how much longer I could put up with it. My dad gave me the best advice a father could ever give. He said, "Don't quit on a bad day, only quit on a good day. If you have a good day and you still want to leave, then you can make that decision, but not until then." It was for that reason that I didn't give up, and I am eternally grateful for that advice. Because I persisted, I had the opportunity to become a leader, which lead me to discover my passion in life and what I'm really good at. I now get to share my passion with many leaders and I love empowering leaders and seeing the relief in their eyes when they discover an easier way.

Then in March 1999, I received some great news. Sixteen months into working for *Great Holiday Escape*, my team leader and 2IC both made the decision to move to a new shop – the same month that the other two novices resigned. This meant that I was the only permanent staff member left in this great big shop, trading six days a week, including from 9am to 9pm on Thursdays and Fridays.

Obviously, I thought this was the best thing that had ever happened and rather than just put my hand up for 2IC, I decided to take a leap and go for the team leader position. My area leader at the time, Alison Crabb, offered me the position on probation by saying, "Okay, you've got three months to prove yourself." So with this, I went about building a whole new team. That was in the day when Flight Centre Ltd didn't have a recruitment team, so here I was, at 22 years of age, interviewing people for the job. The questions I asked were:

1. Do you know how to have fun?
2. Do you barrack for Collingwood (a team in the Australian Football League)?

If you answered yes to both of these questions, you got the job.

Whilst I was working extremely hard and accruing an ever-increasing temp staff bill, I was having a ball. I gathered a great team of people, all with no experience, except for one who came from a travel agent competitor. Three months later, I had a team ready to go – and the shop had lost $50,000 in that financial year.

Being 22 years old and not having any leadership skills, I based all of my leadership on exactly the opposite of what my previous team leader had done. That, along with some great support and advice from my parents, meant that regardless of the lack of experience in our team, we still managed to make $92,000 profit, turning the business around $144,000 and taking out the "Most Improved Great Holiday Escape" award, worldwide.

This was so exciting for us as a team and, as a result, two of my consultants were promoted to team leaders and moved to new shops, which meant recruiting again and rebuilding the team. We did the same process all over again (although I think I had some better interviewing questions this time around) and we started the new financial year as a fresh and excited team! This time around, we made $103,000 profit and achieved "Most Profitable Great Holiday Escape" award, worldwide!

It was at this point that I began looking for what was next, and the area leader position (the role directly above mine) became available. At the ripe old age of 23, I decided that I would apply for it. I was unsuccessful and the feedback was, "Whilst you have achieved in your current shop, you haven't opened a new shop."

So my new area leader at the time asked me, "Where do you want to open a new shop?" The most logical and closest location was a large shopping centre, 3km down the road, so I opened my new store "Escape Travel".

This time around, I employed only novices, so the team I opened the store with had no experience at all. Opening a shop is one of the most challenging things I have done, and to do it on my own with no other experienced consultants, made it ten times harder. I was lucky, however, that one of those novices was an extremely fast learner and became very successful very quickly. We made $64,000 profit in our first full financial year, which is a huge achievement for a brand new shop.

18 months later, the area leader position became available again, and I thought, "Right, I've opened a new shop, surely this one's mine!"

Long story short, again I was unsuccessful and the feedback was, "Yes, you've opened a new store, but you've only ever worked in shopping centres. You need to know what it's like to work in a strip shop (a street frontage shop)."

So, off I went to work in the Central Business District of Melbourne. Here I learned a lot more about leadership that I will share with you later in the book. Essentially, the store wasn't successful and I knew that this all came down to the attitude of the people, which was impossible to change. I wasn't permitted to take action to remove them, so the business continued to lose money.

The area leader position came up again around nine months later, so I thought, "Well, why not apply again? Surely now, with experience in a strip shop, that would cover it!"

Yet again, I was unsuccessful and the feedback this time was, "You don't have enough *business acumen*." I didn't agree with this, because how do you get it without doing it. You can have all the *business acumen* in the world, but if you don't know how to motivate and inspire people on a daily basis, then you will have no numbers to count! I took on the feedback, that I needed to acquire more *business acumen*, and resumed the leadership position I was in.

A few months later, my area leader created a role for me called "High Performance Coach," which involved my visiting all the stores in Victoria to mentor our new consultants in building their business. I loved this role but it didn't fit the Flight Centre model of paying for itself with a clear P&L. Those roles never last long.

After 9 months, I was advised that my role had been made redundant. As this role came to an end, I received a phone call asking if I was going to apply for the area leader position that was currently advertised. I hadn't considered it until then. I did, and again was unsuccessful.

As you can probably imagine, by this stage I was pretty deflated, however, it remained my dream job and I found myself at a crossroads. I loved working for Flight Centre Ltd, but I didn't feel there was any other role that would help me continue my development other than the area leader role. I found myself in a product role and lasted three months. After much angst and consideration, given that even on a good day I wasn't enjoying myself, I handed in my resignation after eight years of employment with Flight Centre Ltd.

While I was the 'High Performance Coach' for Escape Travel, my area leader at Flight Centre had suggested that I look for a qualification in coaching. I researched the industry and found the school for me. It was at an information evening at The Coaching Institute that I met one of the world's most dynamic business women. She opened my mind to so much more than what I was then aware of. I was so excited about this new business opportunity in the coaching industry.

Sharon Pearson was the CEO of The Coaching Institute and I was fortunate enough to be invited into the pilot stages of her Franchise Model. I ran my business for two years, with so many lessons and mistakes, fun and tears.

For example: it took me 5 months to pick up the phone to conduct my first coaching session. I had 20 pages out on the floor to read the questions rather than listen to my client. I was battling my fears of not being good enough, worrying about what others thought of me and dealing with the fear of public speaking when training. It was a steep learning curve.

Two years later, Sharon asked me to join her team and run the business alongside her as the National Operations Manager. I jumped at this chance as I knew that if I was ever going to learn business acumen it was going to be with Sharon.

During this time I learned so much more than I could have ever wished for, and much of my leadership style now comes from the two and a half years I spent with Sharon. I am eternally grateful to this woman for all that she has done for me. Sometimes she pushed me so hard that I didn't like her in the moment, however, in retrospect, those were the moments where I learned the most.

After two and a half years, I was ready for a new challenge and wanted to create something new. She realised that, as the leader of her business and given I was ready for a new challenge, it was time for us to part ways. We parted on great terms and I still remain involved in The Coaching Institute community, referring anyone who asks me about coaching to them.

Upon leaving The Coaching Institute to create my own business, I became aware of the demise of my long-term relationship. This was an extremely difficult time for me and I realised that it wasn't the right time to start my business, both emotionally and financially. So I began working for a software company as a sales person. This gave me the space to rediscover who I was and what I wanted to do with my life.

Roughly five months later, I received a phone call from my old area leader, Alison Crabb, who was now the Nation Leader for the whole state. She said that she would like me to come back to the company as a trainer, with the view of becoming an area leader.

Well, this was the brightest day of the entire previous five months combined. It was like I was called to come home. I was so grateful because, in the midst of what felt like 'my life falling apart', appeared something that I knew was mine. Something no one could take away from me and I knew I was good at it.

Flight Centre.

There was only one problem: I was still beside myself with fear at the thought of public speaking. Whilst I love to train, I would feel physically ill in the moments leading up to a session. However, the idea of obtaining the area leader role was so exciting that I would have done anything to get it, so I felt the fear and did it anyway.

After researching, writing and delivering a series of leadership and sales trainings, I received some great feedback which built my confidence so much that now it's difficult for me to share the microphone when on stage!

Finally, on the 1st April 2011, I was appointed as area leader. I was an area leader for two and a half years and again, grew and developed as a leader through learning what it took to lead 110 people who I didn't have contact with on a daily basis.

The journey as an area leader was incredible and I am privileged to have worked with some amazing people. It was everything I had dreamed it would be and more. And what's funny about my story is that I'm now pleased that I didn't get the job any earlier. All of the experience that I gathered in the lead up really gave me an amazing skillset that I believe has made me a more effective and impactful area leader than I would have been otherwise.

Introduction

I am truly grateful for the opportunity I have had to lead so many amazing and wonderful people. It is a privilege to be the leader of another person. However, having the 'title' of 'leader' isn't what makes you a leader. Anyone can gain or give themselves a title. We can't expect people to respect us just because we have a title, and nor should they. We are all fortunate enough to have the ability to make our own decisions and decide who we will and won't respect and follow.

Generally, people will follow someone who inspires them, who makes them feel good and motivates them to get the results they desire. They will follow someone who leads by example, demonstrates the way, and will *do* whatever they expect from their team. They want to admire their leader, someone who is solid and consistent in the good times and who is even more solid and consistent in the tough times.

I have been fortunate enough to work with some outstanding leaders as well as some less-than-average leaders and it's from this experience, as well as my experience in Life and Executive Coaching using Neuro-Linguistic Programming skills, that I have developed a burning passion to provide a simple step-by-step, clear explanation of how to be a 'motivational leader' for leaders of small and medium sized teams who are looking for a new way.

Regardless of whether the business owner or leader acknowledges it or not, the quality of leadership in any business will have the greatest impact on the bottom line over any other internal factor. A poor leader will cause high staff turnover, unhappy employees, and worse still, unhappy customers, in turn leading to low profits. A motivational leader will ensure high staff retention, happy employees and even happier customers, which in turn leads to ever-increasing profits.

This book is centralised around the leadership model, *Dynamic Leadership Theorem*, which was developed out of a passion and a knowing about what must happen in what order to ensure you are/become a motivational leader and giving you the business results you desire. The six steps in *Dynamic Leadership Theorem* are:

1. Belief
2. Communication
3. Discipline
4. Environment
5. Focus
6. Game Plan

Each step has a series of sub-steps which, when applied, will give the leader the clear and concise knowhow to develop and build a successful team. When this is applied, regardless of what business you are in, you will notice a shift in energy, focus, productivity and, ultimately, profit.

Dynamic Leadership Theorem is focused on the 'soft skills' of leadership and also helps to build the leaders 'emotional intelligence through developing their own self awareness' Whilst emotional intelligence (EQ) and soft skills can have a reputation of being a bit 'fluffy', a leader's skill in this area can, more often than not, be the difference between profit and loss or success and failure in business.

There may be two leaders who run their business doing exactly the same things, yet obtain two totally different results. The difference is their soft skillset: what they believe about their business, how they communicate with their people, the degree to which they are disciplined, what their environment is like, where they direct their focus and what their game plan is.

For example: think of a boss you've had in the past or one you know of who is short and abrupt. They only take the time to speak to you when you've done something wrong or when they need to address your results. Because of their approach, regardless of whether intentional or not, they appear uncaring, heartless and possibly even rude. They may have never taken the time to get to know you as a person and certainly have no idea what's happening in your world. They expect you to respect them because they have a title and use that title as a reason to treat you however they want.

Now, think of a boss you may have had, know of, or would like to be, who demonstrates that they care by taking the time to talk to you, asking how you are and showing genuine interest in your response. They offer constructive feedback and recognize you when you've done a great job as well as when you need to improve. They ask you questions and validate where you're at, then show you how to improve by teaching you a new way. They encourage communication and show respect for you as they expect it in return.

As you can imagine, the environment and culture that these two leaders would create are two very different experiences. The first builds an environment of fear and survival, creating results including, but not limited to, high staff turnover, low productivity, large recruitment and training costs, poor customer service, low customer retention, high marketing costs, and ultimately, low or no profit. It is very difficult, if not impossible, to run a successful and sustainable business in this manner.

The latter fosters an environment of success and empowerment. The individuals feel validated, respected, valued and happy to go above and beyond. When you establish this type of environment, you'll attract great individuals and keep them. This style of leadership increases staff retention, which creates great customer service and high customer retention, as well as reducing recruitment, training and marketing costs. It's very easy to run a successful business when you have created this environment. The challenge is in creating it.

> *When humans are in a fear based environment all they can do is focus on how to survive, thus giving them no room to focus on being successful.*

Dynamic Leadership Theorem (DLT) is all about helping you develop your soft skills and emotional intelligence so that you can learn what it takes to run a successful business, as demonstrated in the second example. When your team can focus on success rather than survival, then, and only then, will you build, develop and retain a successful team, ultimately allowing you to become a successful and motivational leader. Leadership is a learned and developed skill. Whilst some people may be born with attributes that contribute to their effectiveness as a leader, every leader must prioritize their own development to become efficient and effective as a leader in business.

This is NOT A QUICK FIX. Developing exceptional leadership skills isn't an overnight task. It requires focus, dedication and a clear commitment to becoming the best leader you can be. But if you desire to gain long-term, sustainable results, then developing your leadership skills is the only way to do it. It will require you to look at yourself, learn more about who you are and it may, at times, become uncomfortable. You will gain a greater personal awareness and knowledge around who you need to be in order to be a motivational leader. How can you expect your people to be willing to learn and grow if you're not? As the saying goes:

"You're either green and growing, or ripe and rotting."

~ Ray Kroc

Throughout this book, we are going to build your skillset and knowledge around these 6 major concepts – and you will walk away knowing what it takes and, more importantly, HOW to be an amazingly successful and motivational leader! There are six parts to this book, each with a series of chapters and sub-chapters. There will be exercises for you to complete throughout the book, giving you an opportunity to apply the concept in your daily working life to gain a deeper understanding.

It is up to you to follow through with this. One of the biggest pitfalls of leadership is the lack of follow through. However, all it takes is a decision to take action. Make a note to remind yourself during the day. If you apply the learning in this book, you will walk forwards, armed with the knowledge of how to achieve all that you want to achieve as a leader. The choice is yours.

My sincere wish for you is that you gain a deep understanding and a clear step-by-step knowledge of how to become a motivational leader. Leadership is the way of the future. As we embark on a new era of awareness and understanding, businesses will be seeking individuals with outstanding leadership skills to lead and grow their business. Leadership, after all, is one role that cannot be replaced by a computer. Join with me in my mission to create happy people in positive work environments across the globe.

Dynamic Leadership Theorem (DLT) In Detail!

DLT is a model that has been constructed over the past eighteen years. There are different aspects to being a motivational leader: the internal experience and who we are as a person, and the external component, which is how the outside world will experience us.

When looking at the DLT model, it's important to understand that each stage builds on the prior one and should be learned in that order. I am absolutely passionate about not only helping people learn *what* motivational leadership is, but also *how* to be a motivational leader. This is something that I believe is lacking in many training programmes and books, and it's really important to me that you know *how* to be a motivational leader after reading this book.

The DLT model begins with your **Belief.** What you believe is determined by how you think. Your beliefs are what determine your behaviour and how you interact with the world, so it's a must to begin here. We look at what drives you, how your mind works, how you process information and who you *are* on a daily basis. We'll also look at how to adopt a mindset that will help you achieve the results you are looking for.

The next step is mastering your **Communication**, which is all about how a leader communicates and interacts with their staff and customers. As a leader, we have the ability to inspire or deflate our team simply by how we communicate, in all circumstances, from celebrating an achievement to reprimanding a behaviour. One could assume that, as leaders, we want our people to be successful, so knowing how to communicate is essential to help our team achieve their greatest potential. In order to be a successful communicator, we must ensure that we are building on solid and resourceful beliefs.

Once we have mastered communication, we must then ensure we conduct ourselves and our business with internal **Discipline.** This is not discipline as in telling people off, rather being and doing what needs to be done to ensure that the right things happen on a daily basis. It's about learning how to *manage* you, understanding a clear structure, implementing it and holding your people to account. You don't, however, have good discipline without the ability to communicate effectively – because without effective communication, a disciplined environment can be too strict and sterile. Certainly not motivating.

Once you have adopted the discipline principles, you are in a position to focus on developing a positive **Environment.** All of the previous steps are essential to creating a successful environment. Once you've succeeded with the first three steps, you can enhance the creation of this environment by ensuring that your people feel safe and secure. This means they can focus on being successful and achieve through feeling empowered and happy.

Then it's time to **Focus** on doing what needs to be done to achieve the desired outcome. We look in great detail at what it takes to create an effective Business/Team vision, how to set effective goals, take action and finally, what to do if the wheels fall off and how to get back on track.

Finally, we must ensure that the external **Game Plan** matches what your desired outcome is, ensuring that everyone knows what is expected of them at all times. We also look at the power of knowing your numbers and the importance of working 'on', not just 'in' your business. Once you have these six elements of your leadership in place, you will be equipped to run a happy, stable and successful team which will help you achieve what it is you want to achieve.

As I mentioned, I'm passionate about helping you know HOW to apply this, so a simple way to remember this is that it is the beginning of the alphabet:

A is Achieving motivational leader status, you must apply the DLT model to your leadership.

B is for Belief,

C is for Communication,

D is for Discipline,

E is for Environment,

F is for Focusing on the right things, and finally,

G is to develop a clear Game Plan to take relevant daily actions.

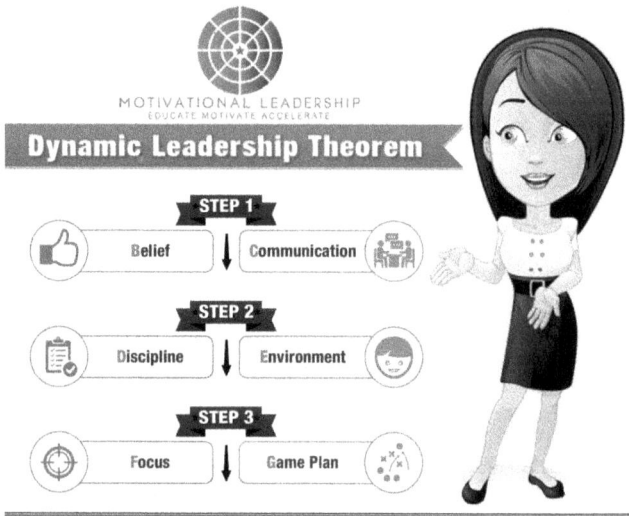

PART 1
Belief

Chapter 1:
The Choices You Make
Are Yours to Choose

"Whether you think you can or you think you can't you are right."

~ Henry Ford

Belief is the foundation of the DLT model. Leadership emulates life. Who we are and what we believe will determine everything we experience in our external environment. If we don't like something in our environment, we can choose to look internally to address what we must change. So it's no accident that Belief is the foundation upon which everything else is built in the DLT model. The Belief section of DLT represents your internal world of who you believe you are, based on what you believe and your personal awareness. It helps you to begin exploring and gain clarity around these complex questions.

In this chapter, we will explore:

- What is your purpose?
- What attitude do you choose?
- Are you an optimist or a pessimist? Which one will help you get your desired results?

The belief section of DLT begins with deciding who you are as a leader by exploring your purpose, choosing your attitude, understanding the difference between being an optimist and a pessimist, and how that choice impacts your results. The more time you spend understanding these concepts, the faster you will progress as a leader. You may find the Belief section of the DLT model a little challenging as it will require you to think differently at times. It's ok to leave a section and return to it, should it not make sense to you just yet.

What Is Your Purpose?

In life, it can be easy to get bogged down into all the problems and drama, both at home and at work. Looking at all the things you need to get done, relationships you need to manage, fitting in with other people's agendas, can get a little overwhelming and, quite frankly, sometimes scary. Nobody, no matter how motivated they are, can remain upbeat and positive if they are constantly focused on the mundane chores of life and business.

This is why knowing and understanding what your purpose is, is crucial to your success as a leader. When you understand why you are doing what you are doing, that there's a bigger picture you're working towards, it makes the tedious tasks more bearable.

Another way to explain 'purpose' is 'the reason why you do what you do'. I say this because in coaching, we have a saying: 'given a big enough reason why, the how will look after itself.' So when you are clear on why you are doing what you are doing, it's easier to push through the tough times. When you push through – and only when you are willing to push through – these times, you will have success. This, I believe, is the key difference between successful people and unsuccessful people. Have you ever met someone who starts something new, gets really excited about it, however maybe six or twelve months into it, will start to flounder and talk about giving up, because it all got too hard?

I choose to believe that such a time is a test for me. This moment in time when it gets tough, or too hard, or whatever I want to call it, is me being tested on my level of commitment. If I'm clear about my purpose and committed to it, I will push through, and if I'm not, I will give up. The key to knowing whether or not you are committed is to know your reason or purpose for doing what you are doing. You can only know that when you know the big picture.

The best example I have is my own experience right now. I have been working on this business for the last two years. The training programme is over 100 PowerPoint slides long, and the book is over 75,000 words. Writing the training programme and book, along with developing the website, has been, at times, tedious with task after task after task, making it feel like it would never end. However, I have been very clear about my purpose from day one: "To inspire and educate leaders who want to learn", whilst spending important valuable time with my brand new baby girl. That is what has powered me through the long late nights to develop this material for you.

When you know your 'why', you have a greater chance of becoming a successful and motivational leader, because all the daily chores and 'things that need to be done' are much more bearable. You know why you have to get them done, you know that there is a big picture and a goal that it's leading you to, and that if you don't take this step, if you don't push through, then you won't achieve this goal.

If you're not clear on your purpose already, I've included some coaching questions that you can ask yourself to begin the process of discovering your purpose:

What are you good at or do with ease?

_____

_____

What do other people say you're good at?

_____

_____

_____

What characteristics or skills to you admire in others? (Because what you admire in others is also within you, and what stands out in others is what you like the most about you!)

_____

_____

_____

What do you want to achieve in the next 5 years, career-wise?

_____

_____

_____

_____

_____

What do you want to achieve in the next 5 years, personally?

_____

_____

_____

_____

_____

_____

How is what you are doing right now, contributing to those goals?

_____

_____

_____

_____

_____

_____

What's important to you about what you do?

_____

_____

_____

_____

_____

What makes you proud of what you do?

_____

_____

_____

_____

_____

_____

If you could do anything you wanted, what would your ideal day look like?

_____

_____

_____

_____

_____

_____

What gets you out of bed in the morning?

_____

_____

_____

_____

_____

What do you want to be proud of at the end of your life?

_____

_____

_____

_____

_____

As you can see, some of these questions will be quite easy for you to answer and some may take a little more time to explore. The more detailed you are with your answers, the more clarity you will gain around your purpose.

Now that you've answered all of these questions, go back over your answers and highlight the words that give you a sense of excitement, a thrill or a feeling of butterflies. The words that you feel passionate about and can see yourself doing for the rest of your life. If you haven't got that yet, then you may need to dig deeper, get into the emotion of *your* answer. There maybe a huge list of words or only one or two. Either way it's perfect. Now summarise these words into a statement of intention, where, if this is how you had to live the rest of your life, you would be ecstatic to do so.

For example: My purpose is "To inspire and educate leaders who want to learn".

I don't mind how I get to do this, whether it be through writing this book, presenting to an audience in a face-to-face training session, or via the e-course I have written. The mode of delivery may be different, however I am still fufilling my purpose of inspiring and education leaders who want to learn.

Now, establish your statement of intention, as your purpose below:

My Purpose is:

_____

_____

_____

_____

The above questions have been designed to start you on the process of discovering your purpose. They are by no means the only way to discover and explore your purpose. It also may not come to you immediately. The answers to these questions may grow and evolve days, and even weeks, after you first answer them. Take your time to work through this process and allow it to unfold naturally, through thought and conversation. This will evolve over time, so enjoy the process.

Should you want some assistance to discover your life purpose, I highly recommend seeing a personal coach, who specialises in 'purpose discovery'.

If you'd like a recommendation, please feel free to email me at lisa@motivationalleadership.com.au.

Attitude Is Simply A Decision

Are you lucky enough to have some positive people in your life? People who are empowered, positive and passionate about life in general. How do you feel when you're around them? Do they inspire you? Would you prefer to spend time with them rather than someone who's not so positive?

Have you ever known someone who has a negative attitude? What is their demeanour? How do they present themselves? Do they come across as people you'd like to spend more time with, people who you'd like to learn from and be inspired by? I'm going to go out on a limb and assume your answer is 'no'.

Let's bring it back to leadership, have you ever worked with or known a leader with a poor attitude? What was your experience? Did you enjoy work? How did you feel as a team member? Were you successful in your role? Did it matter how skilled they were at the technical 'job' they did?

Early in my career, I worked with a leader who constantly displayed a poor attitude. Technically she was great at her job, with customers and the back office tasks – you could tell she really loved doing that. But for some reason, she didn't project a positive attitude to her staff, which meant that she was quite negative all the time and certainly wasn't being a motivational 'leader'. She constantly looked for reasons why we couldn't succeed, made excuses and sometimes only talked to me when I was underperforming. There was always a problem, and therefore the leadership team would snigger and whisper, which made the work environment awfully uncomfortable to be in most of the time.

I believe, as a direct result of the environment I found myself in and being very new and easily influenced by my leader's negative attitude, my results were often poor. I felt bad most of the time because of the environment I was in, however I now know this was mostly because I also chose a disempowered attitude. I didn't know I could take control of my mindset and change my results.

Have you ever worked who has a leader with a great attitude? What was your experience? Did you enjoy work? How did you feel as a team member? Were you successful in your role? I absolutely have and it makes work so much more enjoyable when you're working for a positive leader.

When you work with a leader who is positive, focused on what can be done and has a great attitude, it somehow makes you feel good. You want to work harder and achieve more because you are working together as a team. The Oxford dictionary states that attitude is:

A settled way of thinking or feeling about something.

How you think and feel about something is communicated in your words, your actions, your body language and the way you speak. It's important to be aware of all forms of communication. Ultimately, your attitude will influence your behaviour and your communication and whether you're successful or unsuccessful in life will be determined by how you behave and communicate. As a leader, you are under the microscope; your team is watching your every move. Your words, your actions, your body language and the way you speak, all reflect in your team's attitude and performance.

As their leader, it's easy to forget how much influence and impact you have on your team and the overall environment.

Can you remember what it was like when you first started out in your career? How did you view your direct leader?

Maybe, like me, you thought they were exceptionally important, and everything they said must be true. I totally understand. You as a person haven't changed, yet now, as a leader, you have all these people who look up to you and are watching every move you make. You must respect this position. It's a position of honour, because you hold great power and it's important not to abuse that power. How your people feel about work will be directly influenced by your impact as a leader. The good news is that you have a direct influence on how they feel at work.

An important aspect of adopting the right attitude is ensuring that you behave according to how you expect your people to behave. This is called *integrity*, behaving as you expect your people to behave. Integrity as a leader is crucial for success. If you don't have integrity, your people won't respect you and won't follow you. Ultimately, that means you're not a leader.

Sometimes the easiest way to understand what to do is to look at what not to do first. Let's paint a picture of the worst type of leader with a bad attitude. This is by no means a complete list, simply a scant description of someone who may have a bad attitude:

- The worst thing you can do is reprimand your people for something you do or have done. It's a guaranteed way to lose respect.
- Arrive late and tired.
- Complain about everything.
- Bitch about the company.
- Bag out the customers.
- Can't be bothered demeanour.
- Negative.
- Demonstrate a victim mentality.

After looking at the list of 'what not to do' in attitudes, it gives us a great start in creating a list of what kind of attitude would help you become a motivational leader by simply establishing the opposite. For example:

- Lead by example in not only your attitude, but your behaviour overall. Expect your people to do what you do 100 times and that must be okay.

- Your people will meet you at approximately 80% of what you do. For example: if you arrive to work in the morning with just a "Hello", your people will meet you with a "Hi". If you walk in with a "Good morning, how are you today?" your people may respond with, "Hello, good morning, I'm..."

- Choose to see the positive in each challenge, rather than the difficulty. If a situation arises and you're not happy about it, assess it. Can you do anything about it? If so, do it. If you can't, then deal with it and move on.

- If you are unhappy with the company or a decision that has been made, express that to the people who can do something about it, for example, your leader. Never express it down line to your people.

- The truth is, there will always be difficult customers and there will always be lovely customers. That which you choose to put energy into will be what you get more of. The fact is, without customers you and your team don't have a job. So appreciate them, if for no other reason than they are the ones that give you the opportunity to earn an income.

- Choose a demeanour that communicates what your desired result is. Body language tells our people more about how we feel and what we think than our words do, so be sure to choose body language that communicates what you want your people to know and think.

- Choose a positive attitude that is always possibility and solution focused.
- Demonstrate an empowered way of thinking and focus only on what you have control over. Ask the question: 'Is this something I can control?' If it is, then do something about it, if it isn't then change how you think about it and move on.

In summary, your people will look to you for how to behave and what attitude to adopt. They will learn more from what you *do* than they will ever learn from what you *say*. We will explore many of the above mentioned attitudes as we proceed through the book. The most important aspect of attitude is to lead by example. Whatever you do, it must be okay for your people to do. I have a saying: "If you do it, you're handing them the licence to do it 100 times." Don't think they won't notice. As a leader, you are now under the microscope, and they will notice everything that you do, especially your attitude.

Optimism Vs Pessimism

Have you heard of the 'Law of Attraction'? You may also understand it as the revelation known as the 'Secret' which Rhonda Byrne brought to light in 2006. Regardless of what you call it, it is a law of the universe that many have understood for thousands of years. Essentially, it means that the dominant thoughts and feelings you have will attract, like a magnet, events and situations that help you feel more of those thoughts and feelings.

Wikipedia says that **Optimism** is a mental attitude or world view that interprets situations and events as being best (optimised), so that in some way that may not be fully comprehended, the present moment is in an optimum state. The concept is extended to include the hope that future conditions will unfold as optimal.

Essentially, if you are an optimist, you will look for the opportunity in a situation. You will see the good in it and remain hopeful of positivity in the future.

Wikipedia states that **Pessimism** is a state of mind in which one anticipates undesirable outcomes or believes that the evil or hardships in life outweigh the good or luxuries. Value judgments may vary dramatically between individuals, even when judgments of fact are undisputed.

So, if you call yourself a pessimist, you will typically see the difficulty in a situation, the injustice and, therefore, will feel quite hopeless about the future. Here's the thing: whilst we may have a certain disposition to which way our mind naturally flows, whether you are an optimist or a pessimist is ultimately your choice. I want to introduce you to quite a large statement that could be discussed for days. I'm not going to, but need to share it with you to build on this point.

"Nothing has meaning except for the meaning we give it."

*T. Harv Eker T. Harv Eker wrote about this concept
in his book 'Secrets of the Millionaire Mind'*

There are many different ways to look at the one situation. Regardless of what that situation is – it could be quite trivial or highly controversial – the rule stands. Nothing has meaning except for the meaning we give it. Think about the concept of driving. What do you think about when you think of driving a car? Do you drive? What experience have you had as a driver? Is it a positive or a negative one? All of this will make up what your current perception is of 'driving'.

Answer this question, so you're clear on what your perception is.

_____

_____

_____

_____

_____

Now you're clear on your perception, let's try viewing it from another view point.
How do you think a taxi driver experiences driving?

_____

_____

_____

_____

_____

How do you think a 16-wheeler semi-trailer truck driver experiences driving?

_____

_____

_____

_____

What about a 70-year-old lady?

_____

_____

_____

_____

What about an 18-year-old boy who just got his licence?

_____

_____

_____

_____

_____

What about a driver in Bali or Egypt? (Have you been there?)

_____

_____

_____

_____

What about a 50-year-old lady who's just got her licence?

_____

_____

_____

_____

So, just by looking at the concept of driving, you can see that there are many different perspectives of the same concept. Therefore, every person will assign a different meaning and have a different perception of the same concept. So the question is, who is right?

They all are, aren't they! Because each of them view the concept of driving based on their own experience. Do you think that the taxi driver could learn to view driving like the 70-year-old lady does? Absolutely! Do you think the 18-year-old could learn to view driving like the 50-year-old lady who's just got her licence? Definitely. The question is, do they want to? If they want to learn a different perspective, they need to educate themselves on what that person thinks about, focuses on and tells themselves as they are driving.

It's the same for you as either an optimist or a pessimist. If you want to change your perspective either way, then you must educate yourself on what a person who is an 'optimist' or 'pessimist' thinks about, focuses on and tells themselves. Then, and only then, will you begin to learn and understand what it takes to be an optimist or a pessimist, giving yourself the best opportunity to change your perspective.

Now, it's important to mention here that for every positive to exist, so must the negative. For up to exist, so must down. For right to exist, so must wrong. For good to exist, so must bad. One can't exist without the polar opposite existing. There is evidence for every perspective, and if you search for it, you will find it.

Again, when you relate it to optimism and pessimism, the question is, "Who is right?" The answer is that everyone is right based on the evidence they are searching for. What they think about, focus on and tell themselves will determine what they find. With any situation you experience, in leadership, or life for that matter, seeing the difficulty or seeing the opportunity is simply looking at it from a different perspective. It's the same situation just different perspective.

It's important to remember this when something happens that you would normally react negatively to and become the victim. It's NEVER the situation that is the problem, it's simply what you choose to think about, focus on and tell yourself. Yes, sometimes situations are unpleasant or frustrating. The question is, how does reacting badly to it make it any better? It doesn't, does it? In fact, it just makes it worse.

So as a leader, regardless of the situation, you must choose your perspective carefully, and remain on purpose, as the perspective you choose will most likely be the one that your team chooses. If you fly off the handle and become negative and reactive to a situation because that's your natural default, how do you think your team will respond? They will most likely follow suit. Therefore, the question you must ask yourself as a leader is: "What response/reaction is going to help me get the desired outcome or the results I'm looking for?" Because ultimately, that will be the response your people give and the results they will get as well.

The best way to do this is to ask yourself: "Is this something I can control?" If the answer is 'yes', then do something about it. If the answer is 'no', then why put any energy into it? Just deal with it and move on. When you focus on what you can control, then you still have power and you can change your reaction and behaviour to make the best of a difficult or bad situation.

Chapter 2: Understanding Your Mind

"Turn your face to the sun and the shadows fall behind you."

~ Charlotte Whitton

In chapter two, we'll explore in more depth how your mind works. To master the art of leadership, you must gain great insight and a depth of understanding of how human beings operate. Often, people will demonstrate behaviour that gives them results they don't want, makes them feel bad, unhappy, or even depressed. Being a leader means dealing with people and their emotions. If you know and understand the basics of human behavioural patterns and potentially why people do what they do, then you have the greatest opportunity to help them.

In this chapter, we will explore:

- The Be, Do, Have model.
- Your willingness to take ownership and responsibility for everything.
- The power of your focus.
- Understanding the concept of chunking and how it impacts your communication.

- The three universal fears that drive every person's behaviour on some level.

The beauty of understanding the human behaviour of others is that you also get to learn and apply the concepts yourself. Often it's easier to give advice rather than take it yourself. This is not a tick-the-box style of learning. What you're going to learn in the next chapter is the beginning of an evolution of learning through applying it in your life and leadership. It requires the ability to reflect and refine your learning to gain distinctions in these areas. As I said, this is not learning that you complete and move on. This is something that, if you choose to, you'll focus on and practise for the rest of your life.

"Have, Do, Be" Or "Be, Do, Have"

Society teaches us as children that, "When I have_____ (the goal), then I can be _____ (insert desired emotion here)." When I have the car, the house, the money, the partner, *then* I will be happy. We believe that it's in obtaining something external to us, a material asset or a 'life partner', that will be what's going to make us happy.

Do you know someone who thinks like this? Do you think like this? It's okay if you do, you're quite normal, as it's the common way of thinking that keeps us on the treadmill of life. We work harder or faster in order to progress and earn more money so we can buy the car and the house, and attract the right partner. Do you know of anyone who you believe 'has it all', someone who you think, "Wow, they have achieved it all!" but when you speak to them, you find they are still miserable and complaining about situations in their life or business that make them unhappy?

Generally speaking, most people live their life this way and are miserable. If this is not you, then congratulations, you are one of the minority. If so, then think about this in the context of your people. This is not just a leadership lesson, this is a life lesson. Understanding this means you will be streets ahead of most people in life, because you'll know how to choose to be happy, just with this one key lesson!

The emotions you feel on a daily basis determine your behaviour and actions and determine what your result or outcome is. So, how you feel on a daily basis, will determine your behaviour which in turn will determine your results. If you don't like the results you're getting, you must change the emotions you're choosing, to change your behaviour, which will change your results. You can apply this to anything in life, however because we are talking about leadership, lets look at an example.

A leader is frustrated because his/her team isn't achieving the business goals set. The leader openly communicates this frustration and disappointment. This means the team and the team leader lose confidence and make more mistakes which leads to more underperformance and missed goals. The team leader needs to reverse the thought pattern from 'my results determine how I feel' to understanding that 'how I feel will determine my results'.

The equation looks like this:

Emotions / Being = Actions / Doing = Results / Having

So, the ultimate question to ask yourself, to ensure your being is aligned with the results you are wanting to achieve is:

"Who do I need to be, to do what I need to do, so I achieve and have what I want to have?"

What is the **BEING**?

The being is who you are. It's not a set of actions or a to do list, it's your regular and consistent emotions and characteristics that you display. It's 'who' you are, not 'what' you do.

What is the **DOING**?

The doing is simply the actions you take. It is how you behave, what actions you take consistently.

The **HAVING**?

This requires little explanation. However, the having is your outcome. It is the result you obtain.

The *being* must always come first in this equation, because no matter what you do, unless you *be* the person you need to be, you won't take the action required and you will never have the results you want to have. The great news is that your *being* and *action* are directly in your control. The *having* or the outcome is not. If you can reflect on your results and know that you were being all that you could be and did all you could do, then you can feel positive about the outcome, regardless of the result. It all begins with the *being* which is completely up to you. You can choose what emotions you want to have in any given moment.

For example:

Take a moment to close your eyes. Think about a time in the past, where you experienced true sadness. It's ok, we won't stay there for long. Go back to that time right now, see what you saw, hear what you heard and feel the feelings of what it truly felt like to experience true sadness. Have you got it?

What are you feeling? It may be sadness, it may be fear, it may be apathy. That's ok, the key here is what you're not feeling. Happy? Empowered?

What emotion are you feeling right now?

Did you have pancakes for breakfast?

No?

Ok, we're back.

Now, let's give this another go, but this time I want you to think about a time in the past when you felt extreme elation, happiness beyond measure. Maybe the birth of a child, a wedding day or a holiday you went on. Select a moment in your life when you felt truly happy. Now, go back to that time, see what you saw, hear what you heard, feel the feelings of what it felt like to experience true happiness. Are you there?

Now, let me ask you, what are you feeling now? It may be happy, excited, calm or pleasant. Whatever you are feeling from that moment is perfect.

What emotion are you feeling right now?

The purpose of doing this exercise is to demonstrate to you, that you have access to any one of the 7000 emotions that we humans have access to in any given moment. As you have just experienced, it's simply where you choose to focus. So, given that you can choose your emotions in any given moment, doesn't that pose the question: "What emotions are going to lead me to obtaining the results I want?" This all comes down to your self-awareness of how your emotions impact the rest of your team. Let's take a look.

Who NOT To Be As A Leader:

The best way to describe who you need to be as a leader is to begin with who not to be. I'm sure you would agree that an ugly leader is someone who is judgmental. Someone who criticizes everyone. Someone who needs to put others down for them to feel better or get ahead. Someone who is grumpy and unpredictable with daily mood swings like a see-saw. A poor leader also makes it all about themselves, takes all the credit when things go well and blames everyone else when things go wrong. They turn up late to unplanned, unorganised meetings, run meetings for the sake of running a meeting, or worse still, don't run meetings and don't have any focus. They don't have a team goal and certainly never talk about a team goal.

A poor leader would demonstrate the following Emotions or Characteristics:

No energy, no passion, no focus, no drive, no persistence or determination, uncertain, unclear, rude, obnoxious, arrogant, negative, pessimistic, takes no responsibility, has no ownership, blames and makes excuses for everything. Threatens consequences and never follows through. Is unmotivated and can't be bothered. Money driven, only thinks about and talks about the dollars. Inconsiderate and doesn't validate others' feelings. They demonstrate no self-discipline, which allows others to be undisciplined as well. They speak with a judgemental tone of voice. They are defensive and resistant to change. Essentially, they are the type of people you wouldn't want to be friends with because they offer nothing to the relationship. They are an energy sucker and are a drain to be around.

Who TO Be To Be An Outstanding Leader:

That's a comprehensive list of who not to be and what emotions and characteristics to demonstrate to be a poor leader, now let's take a look at who we need to be and what characteristics and emotions we must demonstrate to be an outstanding leader.

Let's take a look at what it takes to be an outstanding leader. This is, by no means, a complete list, but it will certainly give you the picture. Firstly, they know and understand that it's never about them. In fact, they understand that the last person to be considered in any of their decision making is themselves. It's all about the team and what's best for them. They take full responsibility when the results are poor and pass on all the credit to their people when the results are great. They trust their people, and demonstrate this through their behaviour.

They give ownership and empower their team to make decisions. They see leadership as a privilege to be involved in, and have the ability to impact on so many people's lives. They are grateful for the position and take their role seriously to ensure that they make a positive impact on the lives of their team members.

An outstanding leader will demonstrate the following Emotions and Characteristics:

Full of energy, extremely passionate, focused, driven, determined, purpose driven, persistent and relentless, a never give up attitude, certain and very clear, polite and respectful to everyone, gracious, positive, optimistic, takes complete responsibility and has full ownership on their business. They know that the buck stops with them. They know that excuses have no uses and learn from mistakes, change something and move on. They are motivated and enthusiastic, know that it's important to love the people (both staff and customers) and the money will come, are considerate of others feelings and will validate them whether they agree or not. They are grateful for all the opportunity that lies before them and have a desire to give back, to help others. They are 'forward thinking' and think outside the square.

As you can see, the difference in these two leaders is polar. Now imagine what it would be like to work in these environments. The results from these two teams or businesses would also be polar opposite. The first would be barely existing, have high staff turnover, high recruitment and training costs, low customer retention, high numbers of customer complaints and low profits, if any at all. The second would be thriving, have high staff retention, low recruitment and training costs, high customer retention, high customer satisfaction and high profits.

This is all determined by the emotions and characteristics of the leader, so you can see how powerful you are. The impact you have is far-reaching. The emotions you choose will determine whether that is positive or negative.

ACTIVITY:

When you think about what you would like to achieve as a leader, what comes to mind? Not what do you want the business to achieve; rather, what do you – as a person – want to achieve? Do you know of someone who has achieved this already? (If you can, have a conversation with them and ask the following questions. If you can't, then what do you imagine would be the answers.)

What emotions do they feel on a consistent basis when they think about their people and business, or when they are at work?

_____

_____

_____

_____

_____

What characteristics would they generally demonstrate? (You can use the lists above as a guide.)

_____

_____

_____

_____

_____

What actions would they take each day? Would they be on purpose or go with the flow – see how it goes type actions?

_____

_____

_____

_____

_____

What are their results like?

_____

_____

Success is not about reinventing the wheel, it's about watching the person that has achieved what you want to achieve, looking at how they conduct themselves, assessing what emotions they feel on a consistent basis, looking at what actions they take, and replicating that as closely as you can.

Ownership and Responsibility

There is an aspect of you that is almost like a thermometer for the results of your team or business. It will determine whether you have success and the extent to which you have success. No matter what else you do in your business, unless you have this, you will always struggle. You will simply be working really hard and get no results. It will lead down a very frustrating path where, as a leader, you can become bitter and resentful, and it's all due to one simple thing.

Ownership and **Responsibility**. Yes, those two words we hear over and over again. Sometimes they just blend into the background and I wonder if we actually understand the meaning any more. Many leaders refuse to, or aren't aware of the importance of, taking ownership and responsibility in their business. In fact, in life, we are taught not to take responsibility, so it's hardly surprising. We are taught to blame the media, the government, the boss, the bank or the taxation department for all the problems that exist in our world. Why we don't have enough money, why we can't change our circumstances, why we don't have enough time to spend with our family. We are taught to lay blame on something or someone external to ourselves. The problem with this is, when we lay blame external to ourselves, where is our power to do anything about it?

For the purpose of this explanation, let's look at what taking ownership and responsibility is in leadership. The extent to which both you and your team take ownership and responsibility for your business will be will directly impact on your success. It is a case of one equals the other. I often asked my leaders, if they were to invest $200,000 of their own money – not borrowed, their own, hard-earned cash – would they have done anything different last month? The leaders who say, "No, why would you ask that?" hands-down are the ones who are getting the results. The leaders who ashamedly look down and say 'yes' are the ones who undoubtedly were not as successful and most likely lost money.

So, how do you take ownership of your team and business? The answer to this question really stems back to your being. The emotions you choose to feel and the characteristics you choose to demonstrate. You can't just tick some boxes and then you *have* ownership. It's about who you are *being* as a leader. Essentially, it's how much you care about your business, your team, your success, yourself and how willing you are to let go of being right.

A great way to check in with where you are on this thermometer is to understand the model of "Above The Line Thinking".

Ownership

Accountability

Responsibility

Blame

Excuses

Denial

Understanding this model means you can always tell what your results will be, depending on where your level of thinking is at.

When you are thinking above the line, you are taking ownership and responsibility and you are accountable for your results. You're focused on getting a great outcome rather than needing to be right. When you are thinking below the line, you are blaming others, making excuses and are possibly even in denial of what the truth is. Essentially, you are externalising your result on something outside of you or your business. You are more concerned with being right than you are with getting the desired result.

Some people may have heard of the concept of 'above the line' thinking and believe that it is simply 'positive' or 'negative' thinking. But if you've had a bad day and a situation has really annoyed you, the last thing you want to hear is someone saying, "Just think positive." The truth is, 'above the line' thinking will give you positive results, and 'below the line' thinking will give you negative results. This is because when you blame and make excuses, where is your power to do anything about it? You've given it over to something or someone else. You are essentially the 'victim'.

When you take ownership and responsibility (even if you're not in the mood for it), that is when your power is to do something about it. You can change something, do something different and will get a different result.

In my time as a leader, I've had many tests on my commitment to taking responsibility. Here are a couple of examples:

Case Study 1:

When I first became a leader, I was in a store that was extremely busy. We were in the heart of a major shopping centre and we had customers visiting us from the moment we opened the doors to the moment we closed them, every single day. It was a pumping, thriving, successful business. When I left it, the team was successful and the customers were happy. I had been there for 5 years, so it was time to move on for a new challenge.

For my second business, I opened a brand new store, with a brand new team. They were learning the skills of the job as well as helping me build the business from scratch. It was a challenging gig. My clients would come in and say, "Wow, it's not as good a location as the last store." As you could imagine, I was delighted with this sprinkle of positivity in front of my brand new team (please note the sarcasm there). I knew they were all listening for my response, for whether or not that meant they couldn't be as successful as the last team. I would reply with, "Oh no, it's fantastic," and pointed out all the reasons I could come up with as to why it was a great location.

Was the location a poor choice? Well, that was irrelevant because I couldn't do anything about it. I couldn't physically pick up the store and move it to the centre of the food court. So, I had to look at other ways to get our name out there and become known in the community.

It would have been much easier to continue as I was in the previous business, just waiting for people to walk through the door and throw money at us, but we wouldn't have got the results we were looking for if we chose that plan of action.

So, it meant we had to take ownership and responsibility for the present situation and think outside the square. It certainly meant we had to do different things compared to what I did in my previous business. We had to get the word out there that we had opened. We did endless amounts of local marketing activities with lots of specials and discounts, almost to the point we were shouting it from the rooftop.

If we had have blamed the location, sat back, waited and complained about the situations that were beyond our control, what do you think our results would have been?

Taking responsibility and ownership for what we could control was the key to our success. We focused on what we could do, took action and as a result, we achieved our desired outcome: Profit!

Case Study 2:

Much later in my career, I was working with a team leader who I truly believed in. I had full faith that she could do this job and do it well. She gave me all of the indicators to let me know that what I'd suggested to her, she was doing in her business and that she wanted it just as much as I wanted it for her. I was getting feedback from reps and trainers who would visit the store, saying, 'the vibe in there is amazing', yet they still weren't making money. I was almost out. I'd suggested and coached and guided everything I could possibly think of. I was running out of ideas to help, but I kept saying to her, "If you keep turning up, we'll figure it out, it may not happen straight away, but it will happen."

A month after I was almost out of ideas, she handed in her resignation. Her feedback was, "You control me too much, I'm scared of you, you don't give me ..., you, you, you." Essentially meaning, "You help me/speak with me/call me too much." To begin with, I was dumbfounded. If anyone asked me which team leader I have really worked with to help increase their leadership skills, to improve their results, I would have said this team leader. I was upset. I couldn't believe the conversation we had, upon her resignation, as I had only ever wanted to help her be successful.

Later that day, I caught up with a coaching friend of mine as I had to digest the information I was given and I couldn't believe that this was real. Let me just say that the response I wanted to give was, "Well, that's her problem, she was no good as a leader," which I now believe to be true, but if I had stopped there, I wouldn't have learned anything out of the whole situation and certainly wouldn't have grown as a leader myself.

The first part of the learning for me (and now hopefully for you) is that it wouldn't have mattered what I did for this team leader. I could have flown to the moon and back, it still wouldn't have been right. She did not take any responsibility for her own success and the success of her team. And nothing anyone else did for her would have helped. I know that the feedback she gave her last area leader was that she didn't *get* enough support. No matter what anyone else did for her, how they led her, she was never going to get any kind of result because she did not take ownership and responsibility for herself, her actions or her team.

The second part of this learning was the gold for me. From this situation over a period of a month, I had a significant defining moment for me as an area leader with my team leaders. I realised that I was micro-managing 16 team leaders.

To an extent, what she'd said was right. I was trying to be the team leader for 16 stores. No wonder I was exhausted. As soon as I realised this, I acknowledged it to my team leaders, metaphorically gave them back their businesses and apologised. It certainly wasn't my intention, but my enthusiasm and desire for them to succeed had taken over.

This is a great example of how our leadership and issues in our 'outside' world are simply a reflection of what's going on in the 'inside' world. It took me a while to find the balance between wanting to control in order to get the best results for them, and being available to support the team leaders as they required. Once I did, there was certainly an incredible shift in results, where we significantly increased some of our major KPI's month on month from the prior year.

Taking responsibility for this situation and owning what happened, as difficult as it was at the time, meant that I was able to gain an even deeper insight into what it meant to be an effective leader, and for that, I'll be eternally grateful to her.

I guess the key here is to let go of the need to be right and not be attached to your ego. Ego is an ugly thing in leadership. When you step up and take responsibility for EVERYTHING that happens in your business, that's when you will propel your growth and development as a leader. People think that when you have a title as a 'leader', that you're meant to know everything, do everything perfectly and never make a mistake. This is a load of hog-wash, and if you think this as a leader, then you will never be an effective leader. As Simon Sinek put it so well, "The biggest mistake many leaders make is thinking they have to know all the answers or thinking that if they don't, they have to pretend they do. One of the biggest failures of most leaders is the belief that their leadership credibility comes from intelligence. It doesn't."

It comes from your experience and willingness to learn from your mistakes. From working towards your vision and your desire to see your people achieve, the absence of an ego and being willing to admit when you're wrong. All of which we will discuss further.

Sometimes, people think that to take responsibility for *everything* means that *everything* is your fault. There is a difference between responsibility and fault. Fault implies blame. This is not about blame, rather taking responsibility, so that you can do something about it to change the outcome in the future.

To be a motivational leader, choose to take complete responsibility for everything that happens in your business, then, and only then, will you have the ability to change your outcome and results in the future.

Where's Your Focus?

When you think about your career and the goals you want to achieve, what do you think about? Take a moment now to get clear on what you want out of your career.

_____

_____

_____

_____

_____

How clear are you on what you want to achieve? Was it easy to write down? Did it come naturally to you, like writing down the names of your direct family members, or did you have to think a little about what you'd like to achieve?

The first step to achieving what you want is to know what you want. That which you are comfortable with and can relay easily, off the top of your head without even thinking about, will be what you get in life.

Imagine for a moment being out in nature, in a clearing in the country. There are mountains in the distance to your right; they are quite tall and picturesque. If you turn your head to the left, you can see an amazing waterfall, cascading down into a beautiful lake, fog hovering over the water and beautiful flowers and trees on the far side. Both in front of you and behind you is green grass as far as the eye can see, until the ground meets the horizon.

Now, imagine holding a telescope up to your eye. You point it in the direction towards the mountain. What can you see? What do you not see? If you point the telescope towards the mountain, you're going to see the mountain, aren't you? You wouldn't see anything else? You certainly wouldn't see the waterfall. Now, turn the telescope towards the waterfall, and what do you see? What can't you see at this moment? If you point the telescope towards the waterfall, you're going to see the waterfall and nothing else. You're certainly not going to see the mountain.

What you focus on, is what you get, and
you exclude everything else.

When we talk about focus it is evident in our language, whether we are focused on what we want or focused on what we don't want. We may feel that we are absolutely focused on what we want, however our language may tell us otherwise. If we are focused on what we don't want, then we'll find lots of 'negative' or 'moving away' language in what we've written.

For example: *don't, fail, limit, lose, no, not, never, quit, reduce* or *stop*.

"I don't want to fail."

"I don't want to lose money."

"I want to lose weight."

"I don't want to work in an unsuccessful business."

"I want to quit sugar."

"I never want to get stressed."

The problem with 'moving away' language is that even though you're clear that you want to 'lose weight' or 'never want to get stressed', where are you focused? On the weight and getting stressed, isn't it? You're certainly not focused on healthy eating and exercise, or meditating and doing yoga when you read those words, are you? The problem with articulating your goals this way is that the 'unconscious' mind doesn't process the negative word. So, when you say "I don't want to get stressed", your unconscious mind hears "I want to get stressed" – leaving the 'don't' out of the instruction and searching for more reasons to feel stressed.

It's like when you tell a child, "Don't spill the milk," or, "Don't touch that." What do they do? They spill the milk and touch that. That's the instruction they hear, so they do it.

Now, imagine that telescope in the context of your goals. If you focused the telescope on what you don't want and/or all the reasons why you couldn't achieve your goals, what would you see? What wouldn't you see? You would be focused on what you don't want and would see all the reasons why you can't achieve it.

If you focused the telescope on your goals and the reasons why you can achieve them, what would you see? More importantly, what wouldn't you see? You would be focused on your goals and would see all the reasons why you could achieve them. You certainly wouldn't see all the reasons why you can't.

Let's review what you wrote at the beginning of this section. What are your goals? If you've written down exactly what you want, then fantastic, well done, you're heading in the right direction. If you've noticed that you've written down what you don't want, then it's okay. It is now time to make a shift and re-word it to what you do want.

This may take a little bit of thinking. Even though it sounds obvious, sometimes it doesn't always come that easily. Simply knowing this means you're more than half-way to changing it. Persist with it, it's worth it.

A great way to approach this is to put it into a vision statement. A vision statement is a statement about what your life/career looks like once you've achieved your desired goals on a given date in the future. It doesn't have to be specific or measurable. This is simply what your picture of success looks like to you.

The most important aspect of writing a vision statement is that it makes you feel good. When you read it, it makes your heart flutter, gives you butterflies in your tummy and goose bumps on your skin.

For example: It is the 31st December, 2020, and I'm elated that I have now achieved global status as an International Trainer and Author on Leadership. I have a waiting list of companies wanting to work with me and many of my heart's desires have been answered. I feel immense love and gratitude as I stand on the deck of my gorgeous home with my family and friends admiring that perfect Melbourne view.

My Vision Statement:

_____

_____

_____

_____

_____

It's important here to revisit something I mentioned in the optimism vs pessimism section: the law of attraction, simply described as a magnet for all you think about and focus on. Whatever you think about, focus on and talk about is what you will attract more of.

Now, whether you like it, understand it, agree with it or not is irrelevant. It's like any other law of the universe. For example: the law of gravity. You don't have to like it, understand it or agree with it to know that if you drop a pen, it's going to fall to the ground. You don't need to understand the physics behind it, what causes it to fall, or any other level of detail to know that it will happen every single time you drop that pen. In fact, there will never be a time when it doesn't fall, will there?

Your feelings and your focus are exactly the same. The law of attraction is the magnet which brings to you more of what you are thinking, feeling and focusing on. The more you feel a certain emotion or focus on a certain outcome, the more likely you are to attract more reasons to feel that emotion and create that certain outcome.

As I alluded to before, our language creates our reality. What we speak about is what we bring about. It's important to be aware of the power of our language so we are aware of what we are bringing into reality.

Imagine that there is a direction that your words travel once they are spoken. They are either focused on and moving towards what you do want or they are focused on and moving away from what you don't want. There is a big difference in the energy of the words we use and the results they create. Whether we like it or not, our team members and our unconscious mind will pick up on the energy of how we speak and go about following instructions (Our unconscious mind will most likely be more obedient than our people, however that's where it all begins). If it's constantly negative and moving away from what you don't want as a leader of a business, then it will impact the energy and the atmosphere of your team, leading to a possibly negative and uninspired environment. Ultimately, this costs you money on the bottom line

Practise speaking words that represent 'towards what you do want', stating it in the positive. For some of us, in the beginning, this can be quite unfamiliar or uncomfortable. Most people are aware of what they don't want, but when you ask them what they do want it's not always so easy to articulate.

It takes a conscious decision to start thinking and talking about what you want in 'towards' language. The great news is that all you need to do is be aware of it consciously and begin correcting yourself as you hear yourself speak in 'away' language. The more you practise this, the better you will get at it. It will make a profound impact on not only your results, but your whole life.

The Importance Of Gratitude In Focus:

Have you ever met someone who is constantly angry or sad, and whilst they may have moments of happiness, it's just a fleeting moment of happiness or they find a problem with the happiness to feel sad about?

It also works in reverse. Do you know of someone who is constantly happy? No matter what seems to be going on, they have always got a smile on their face. Whilst they would also have things that go wrong, it's just a fleeting moment of anger or frustration, and they will find the positive in that situation.

It's no accident as to why this happens. Like I mentioned in the previous section, it's because the feelings they feel on a consistent basis are magnets for more of those feelings.

I want to give you my best tip for choosing to feel the positive rather than the negative. No matter what happens, there is always someone worse off than you. Now, I know that there are some pretty rough things that happen to people and I know that you could think up the worst possible event. What I suggest is to keep this in mind, because if you use this theory, you will not experience the worst of the worst, you will experience only the best of the worst.

The tip is GRATITUDE. Yep, it's as simple as that. Choose to be grateful for an aspect of the event, what you can learn from it, what you still have, no matter how much or how little. Feel the feelings of gratitude on a daily basis for all that you do have.

The more feelings of gratitude you feel, the more you will have to be grateful for. This is not something you just do for 5 minutes and when nothing changes, you give up and say, "That doesn't work." This is something you choose, regardless of what you get out of it. The thing is that most of us have a roof over our head, we have the opportunity to work in a business, we have loved ones around us, we have friends to spend time with, we may even live in a country that gives us the freedom to choose. We are the lucky minority.

If you think about and focus on what you don't have, what you are missing out on or the misfortunes you have to put up with, how do you feel? You begin to feel negative feelings and feelings of lack. Your dominant feeling is 'bad'. The more you indulge yourself in this way of thinking, the more 'bad' feelings you will create and will attract more reasons to feel bad.

Now, compare that to how you feel when you are thinking about the things you have to be grateful for in life, as mentioned above. You feel more positive, happy and empowered. Not only will you attract more reasons to feel this way (I remind you of the "Be, Do Have" model) what you feel will ALWAYS determine what you do, which will then lead you to your outcome or results. So, choose to be grateful with what you do have. If you don't do this already, it will change your whole world.

ACTIVITY:

Start a gratitude journal. Take a new exercise book and write down 20 things you are grateful for every day. This doesn't have to be complicated. Here are some examples of some things most of us can be grateful for today.

1. I am grateful for the air I got to breath today.
2. I am grateful that I opened my eyes this morning.
3. I am grateful for the roof I have over my head.
4. I am grateful for the food I was able to eat today.
5. I am grateful for my improving health.
6. I am grateful for the opportunity I had to learn today.
7. I am grateful for the warmth I felt.
8. I am grateful for the clothes I wore.
9. I am grateful for my friendships.
10. I am grateful for the sun rising today.

The more you make this a daily practice, the easier it will become.

If you want to take it to another level, find a nice looking rock or stone, or any item for that matter, that appeals to you and makes you feel good. Carry it with you everywhere, and every time you touch it, come across it, see it, make it a trigger to take a moment to identify what you're grateful for and be thankful.

Every time you write in your journal, hold it in your hand as you write it. Allow it to soak up the energy of your gratitude. This item will become a symbol of all that you have to be grateful for and will be a consistent source of positivity for you.

Understanding The Concept Of "Chunking"

Do you prefer the big picture, or the detail? Each individual has a preference as to what size unit of information they are comfortable with. It is vital to understand this as a leader because, when you do, not only will you give yourself the best opportunity to be an effective and powerful leader, you will also give your people the best opportunity for success. It will help you to categorise information and give you the ability to remove the word 'overwhelm' from your vocabulary. It will also help you to understand how to motivate yourself and your team, to take action on the things that you procrastinate about.

The concept of 'chunking' was first written about by Harvard psychologist George A. Miller in the 1950's when he published a journal article, *The Magical Number Seven, Plus or Minus Two*. He researched and studied the short term memory and its ability. 'Chunking' is the theory that we can only remember seven plus or minus two pieces of information. The more complex the material, the lower the number of chunks remembered.

Chunking can be easily explained when you are talking about phone numbers. If you had to remember the numbers 2–7–4–0–4–2–6–5, it would be difficult to remember, but if you were to read them as 2740 4265, like a phone number, you would have a greater chance of retaining this information because you're remembering two bigger units of information rather than eight units of smaller information. Where some people prefer to work with large units of information, others prefer to work with much smaller units. Chunking is the size of the unit of information you are talking about. The smaller units of information are contained in the larger units of information.

In this example, we will start with a larger chunk of information and work down to the detail.

Chunk of Information	Explanation – Abstract to Detail	Example questions to ask to chunk down into the detail
Movement	Movement is a large chunk of information because there are many things that can fit into the category of movement.	What specifically are you talking about?
Transportation	Transportation is more specific but is still a large category as there are still many things that fall under the category of transportation.	What is an example of this?
Car	A car is an example of transportation and is beginning to give us a clear picture on what it is we are talking about. It's becoming more specific.	What specific type of car are you referencing?
Mercedes	It's a specific type of a car, isn't it? So that is a smaller unit of information than 'car'.	What is an example of a Mercedes?
SLK 500 Convertible Mercedes	It's an example of a Mercedes, so is a smaller unit again, giving us more information and more detail for a clearer picture.	What specifically do you mean?

Black SLK 500 Convertible Mercedes	Now, even if you don't know exactly what one of these cars looks like, you can still build a reasonably clear picture in your head of what is being spoken about.

So we've established 7 chunks of information, each became smaller and more specific in detail, giving a clearer more detailed picture of what is being spoken about. You could continue further by asking about the interior, leading to the steering wheel or the accelerator, specific units or 'chunks of information' about the car. Having this knowledge as a leader is crucial to helping both yourself and your team members to achieve.

If you have a team member who is finding it difficult to get started on a project or is focused on a problem that is preventing them from moving forward, then you can use this model to help them gain clarity around what is preventing them from moving forward. Asking questions suggested in the third column, like, "What specifically are you talking about?", "Can you give me an example?" or "How specifically will you get this done?" are all examples of questions that you can ask to help someone gain clarity about the tasks that need to be completed.

If it is a project or a problem that you are talking about, then the name of the project or problem will be abstract (a large unit of information).

Your goal is to help them get to the detail of what actions or tasks must be completed in order to get to the end of the project or resolve a problem. The key is to keep asking the questions until they gain a clear picture of what task must be completed first. Once you get them to the first task, then you can ask, "What else must be done?" Continue to ask these questions until they have a clear, action plan which they feel confident to implement.

For example:

Chunk of Information	Explanation – Abstract to Detail	Example questions to ask to chunk down into the detail.
Unhappy team member	'Unhappy' is a large chunk of information because there are many things that can fit into the category of unhappiness.	What specifically are you talking about?
Not achieving my goals	'Not achieving my goals' is more specific, but is still a large category as there are still many things that fall under the category of 'goals'.	How, specifically, do you know you're not achieving your goals?
Not on track this month to my KPI's.	'Not on track to KPI's' falls under the banner of 'not achieving goals' and is beginning to give us a clear picture of what it is we are talking about. It's becoming more specific.	What specific KPI are you referencing?
My Sales	Is now highlighting what the actual problem is. So that is a smaller unit of information than 'Not on track to my KPI's'	What is concerning you specifically about your sales?

I haven't made a sale yet	Is a smaller unit of information again, giving us more information and more detail for a clearer picture.	What specifically do you think is causing this?
My conversion rate is terrible.	Now, you have highlighted what the specific problem is, you can help them with actions to take, to improve, rather than dealing with the ambiguity of 'unhappy'.	

Quite often, even the team member you're talking to, may not be aware of what the specific problem is and by following this line of questioning and helping them become more specific about what they're unhappy about, will make them feel relieved and more positive about potential solutions.

Let's reverse it. In this example, we'll start with the detail and 'chunk up' to the abstract information.

Chunk of Information	Explanation: Detail – Abstract	Example questions to ask to chunk up in order to gain the big picture
Black SLK 500 Convertible Mercedes	This is a very specific picture about what we are talking about. There is a great deal of detail and leave little room for interpretation.	What is this an example of?
SLK 500 Convertible Mercedes	It's an example of an SLK 500 Convertible Mercedes which could be any colour.	For what purpose was this built?

Mercedes	It was built because Mercedes wanted to release a luxury convertible car.	What is a Mercedes an example of?
Car	It's an example of a car.	For what purpose would you want a car?
Transportation	You would want a car, if you were interested in a mode of transportation.	What is transportation an example of?
Movement	Transportation is an example of movement.	

If you find that a team member is overwhelmed, then you will also find that they are stuck too much in the detail, focusing on the endless actions and tasks that must be done on a daily basis, with no end in sight. This is commonly known as 'overwhelm'. If they have too many tasks, then you might need to help 'chunk' them up to remember why they're doing these tasks so they can work more efficiently. If this is the case, it's time to remind them why it is that they've got all these tasks to complete.

You do this by simply asking the question, "For what purpose must you get this done?" or "What is this small project an example of?" or "What is this going to give you?" You keep asking these questions until they realise that, whilst the task may be mundane, it is ultimately leading them to their/the team's 'big picture' or 'vision – the desired outcome'. When they remember 'why' they're doing something, then it makes all the small mundane daily tasks bearable.

Chunk of Information	Explanation: Detail – Abstract	Example questions to ask to chunk up to gain the big picture
Too much on my to-do list	This is a very specific picture about what we are talking about. There is a great deal of detail and leaves little room for interpretation.	What is this an example of?
Pressure and intensity at work	It's an example of the feeling of pressure and intensity.	For what positive purpose would we want pressure and intensity?
To work at a fast pace	Pressure and intensity are components of, so are contained within 'working at a fast pace'.	For what purpose would you want to work at a fast pace?
To achieve our KPI's	'Working at a fast pace' is one way of achieving KPI's, so is contained within.	For what purpose would you want to achieve your KPI's?
To achieve success at work	Achieving KPI's is a component of 'achieving success at work'.	For what purpose would you want to achieve success at work?
To achieve our vision	A vision is a very big chunk of information and represents why your business exists. If you were to go one step further the answer would possibly be 'to be happy', which is usually the biggest chunk you can get to.	

It comes down to what perspective your team member has, and sometimes if they are choosing a highly detailed perspective you simply need to remind them of 'why' they are doing what they are doing. Asking them the above questions, is the best way to help shift their perspective, as they own the answers to the questions you ask and can't help but change the way they see their situation.

So in summary, there are different sized units of information that we are comfortable with and therefore communicate in, the smaller units of information will be contained in the larger ones. If you do overwhelm a lot, then typically you prefer to deal in detail more and need to focus on the bigger picture of 'why' you are doing all these smaller tasks. If you have lots of great ideas but rarely get any of them started, then you prefer the bigger picture and must practise getting more specific about the necessary actions required to achieve the desired outcome.

The key to being a successful leader is to understand this and get great at dealing in both the big picture and the detail. This gives you the ability to listen to people talking and hear what chunk level they're at so you know how to help them move forward with the above suggested questions.

What Are Your People Afraid Of?

Before I started the coaching part of my career, I had very little awareness of my 'self'. If someone asked me "How can I be a great leader?" I would have had no idea how to answer that. My best response would have been, "You just do." I also decided, somehow, that I achieved my greatest success in the first couple of years when I was younger and the older I got, the less likely I would be successful. I even struggled to type that, because I look at that now and think how ridiculous that sounds, but I'm sharing this with you for a reason.

71

You know that voice inside your head, the one that is trying to hold you back, tell you you're not good enough, you'll never be as good as that other person. Well, I believed that I was the only person in the world that had that voice. Like I was the chosen one or something. It was saying, "You're not good enough, you can't have that success again."

When I started coaching, one of the very first and coolest things I learned was that everyone has this voice. Wow, did I feel liberated. Because before coaching, I had decided that successful people didn't have that voice and then the rest (the unsuccessful people) did have that voice. So learning that everyone has it and the only thing that separates the successful people from the unsuccessful people is whether or not they listen to that voice was amazingly liberating.

That voice inside your head can have many names, but most commonly is known as the 'ego'. The ego wants to make sure you get everything perfect, you don't make a mistake and that you are never seen as weak. Its intention is to keep you 'safe'.

There is a part of the brain known as the amygdala. Now, I'm not the most technical person, so here it is in layman's terms. The amygdala is responsible for the perception of emotions, such as fear, anger or sadness. The amygdala will store the memory of an event that triggered a certain emotion so you can easily recognise similar events in the future that may trigger the same emotion, with the intent of self-preservation.

Most people have at least one fear, and many have more than one. We may be fearful of dying, have a fear of public speaking or a fear of heights, for example. Or it may be an internal fear, fear of not belonging, not being good enough or not being loved. Whatever it is, ultimately when the amygdala detects the possibility of experiencing that fear in a situation, it's purpose is to keep you 'safe' from experiencing that fear. In ancient times, when physical safety was a challenge in day to day life, the amygdala was a very useful tool to have, keeping you out of harm's way from predators and any physical threats. In this day and age, it's no longer an immediate necessity. Most of us are not put into life-threatening situations on a daily basis.

The amygdala has evolved to generalise any situation where we perceive that fear or a lack of safety through our own vulnerability and wants to keep us safe by avoiding any situation that would evoke that fear in the future. When it does perceive this fear, that's when our ego fires up and starts 'chattering' because it believes there is something to be fearful of. The possibility of making a mistake, appearing wrong amongst our peers, embarrassing ourselves, is enough to fire off the amygdala and set the ego chattering away in our mind, trying to tell us, "I'm not good enough" or "How can I possibly think that I could achieve that?" Whether we like it or not, it happens to all of us. I've had it as I've been writing this book. "Who's going to want to read this?" and "Really, are you really going to put this out there?" has, at times, been the voice inside my head.

What I've learned along the way is that if you dream it, you can do it. The only thing that's stopping you is you. Your persistence, your determination, and whether you listen to that voice or not. The best way I've learned to dim that voice so far, is to tell myself, "It's my job to do my best work, not to judge whether others will accept it or not. That's up to them." So I'm committed to doing my best work, that's all I must focus on. Another great response to that voice is to say, "Thanks for your input, now be quiet, I'm moving forward anyway." Know that its only intention is to keep you safe, and no-one ever achieved amazing things inside their comfort zone.

There's another factor at play that can have a significant impact on our willingness to step outside our comfort zone, which happens early in our development as human beings. When we are born, from the age of zero to seven years old we experience a stage in our development known as the 'imprinting period'. This is a time of life where we have no 'critical faculty' or in other words, we don't know to question authority. Any person that holds a position of authority in our lives, we will take on and believe what they tell us or communicate to us without question in any event or circumstance.

These figures of authority could be our parents, our teachers, our sporting coaches, even our older siblings. This doesn't have to be a significant event; it can be something quite basic and harmless. These events are known as defining moments. Let me give you an example.

One of my defining moments was when I was 4 years of age. My mum had just had my sister. She must've only been a few weeks or months old (difficult to remember as I was only 4). For some unknown reason, I didn't want to get in the car. She'd put my sister in the car and was calling me to get in the car. But I didn't want to go. So she locked me in the house and said, "Okay, we'll go without you." She drove up the drive way and I watched her, through all my tears and screams, disappear out of sight. I was beside myself for what must've only been a matter of seconds, because she turned around immediately and came back to get me. What else was a mother of a newborn supposed to do? I'm sure all mums out there can empathise.

As a result of this moment, I 'generalised' or 'decided' that I wasn't worth it or I wasn't good enough and then generalised that to mean that in order for me to be equal, I had to be the best. From this moment on, everything I did had to be the best for me to be equal.

I can see evidence in my life all the way through of when I've lived by that:

- I had to be the captain to be equal at school.
- I had to win the tournament to be equal at tennis.

- I was placed in a smaller brand – Great Holiday Escape – and I had to be the most successful to be equal to the Flight Centre Consultants.

There are endless examples of this that demonstrate my 'decision' that I wasn't good enough.

We all have many defining moments throughout our childhood that have caused us to make decisions about ourselves, the world around us and how life is. In fact, some researchers say that once we hit the age of seven, we never make a new decision again. It's always influenced or generalised around an original decision we made about ourselves as children. This is why coaching is so valuable.

As I alluded to before, as human beings, there are three universal fears and all fears are born from one of these three. EVERY single person on this planet has a level of at least one of these fears.

These 3 universal fears are:

- Fear of not belonging.
- Fear of not being good enough.
- Fear of not being loved.

This is the fear that many people allow to control them, holding themselves back from what they truly want to do/achieve because of a fear of rejection, a fear of standing out too much or fear of failure.

As I mentioned before, generally we no longer have a need for the amygdala to keep us physically safe, so it generalises any event that is vaguely familiar to a stored memory of fear and fires off the fear emotion again in anticipation of the need for self preservation. A common example is when a situation arises that we haven't experienced before, and don't know how it's going to turn out. It's outside of our comfort zone and therefore our amygdala determines we must be 'fearful' of the unknown.

But the question is, whoever has had a 'guarantee' of success? Has anyone ever gone out to achieve something that they've never done before and had a guarantee? Not one person has ever had that.

Richard Branson took action, not knowing how things would turn out with the Virgin brand. Kylie Minogue started acting, having no guarantee of where she would end up. Oprah Winfrey took action without having any experience or knowledge of what she was going to create.

Your success is beyond your comfort zone. Successful people are those who take action, regardless of the fear they feel, because they have a passion to achieve something bigger than the 'fear' that could hold them back. I want to share this with you because this is essential to understand as a leader. One of the greatest paralysers of a leader is the fear of change or fear of stepping out of your comfort zone.

So whenever you feel 'scared' or 'fearful' and don't want to do something, be sure to assess the risk vs reward factor. Ask yourself, "What is the risk here, what's the worst that could happen?" Give yourself a reality check. "Am I going to burst into flames?" or "Am I going to explode into a million little pieces?" If the answer is 'no', and your physical safety isn't threatened, then I encourage you to go for it. Now assess the potential reward. What is the best possible outcome? Is it worth it? Because it's only when you push through your comfort zone barrier and get into the 'learning' zone that you will grow and develop as a leader and a human being.

I will share with you one of the many times where the fear of being out of my comfort zone played out. Like many people, one of my greatest fears has always been that of public speaking. When I was coaching, a part of my business was to run training sessions/conferences. I was lucky enough to score what could have been a lucrative opportunity through a friend to present to a rather large company, which I'll be forever grateful for.

Let's just say, it couldn't have gone any worse if I tried. I left the handouts in my car and had to get my keys out of my bag and explain where my car was and were it was in my car in front of 50 people – all staring at me whilst I dealt with my incompetence. It was awful. It was the most horrible experience. I was deeply sorry and apologetic to the business owner and my friend. Did I burst into flames? No. Did I explode into a million little pieces? No. But did I learn to be much more organised and prepared? Absolutely, I learned to prepare and know my content more thoroughly and have I ever done anything like that again? NO!!!! In fact it was this very event that built my strength as a trainer as I learned to improvise and work with what I've got and make that the value.

Training is now one of my favourite things to do; in fact, it's my passion. I have received some amazing feedback from the trainings that I have written and run and I love being in front of a group that I know I can teach, inspire and empower.

So next time you feel fear, with no physical threat, acknowledge the voice inside your head and take action anyway. It may well be the very thing that lights you up and helps you achieve your ultimate purpose, like it was for me.

Chapter 3: Laying the Foundations

"Leadership is practised not so much in words as in attitude and actions."

~ Harold S. Geneen

When you want to gain clarity and certainty about who you are as a leader, it's important to take the time to understand how you as a leader will make decisions and respond in challenging situations. Because anyone can be a 'great leader' in the good times, it's those who stand up and make the powerful and insightful decisions in the tough times who stand out as true leaders. In order to stand firm and be sure about your decisions, you must be clear on two things:

- The vision for your business/team.
- How to make profitable decisions from the heart.

Your response in any given situation, especially a challenging one, will either make or break your success as a leader because it will determine whether your people can trust you or not. So it's crucial that we look at how we respond to feedback to ensure that we can see:

- Feedback is the breakfast of champions.

Once you have acquired the understanding of these three components of your leadership, and how they are the umbrella, encompassing your entire leadership style, you are then ready to move into looking at the power of your communication.

Getting Started On Your Vision

Having a vision is like having a road map with a pinpointed destination when you go on a road trip. If you have one, you know which turns to make, what sign posts you are looking for along the way, how to navigate around the hurdles and bumps and remain on track to the end destination. If you get lost it will help you reconnect with the journey that is leading you to your destination.

Imagine getting in your car with nowhere to go, no destination in mind. Where would you end up? What direction would you travel? Which way would you steer the steering wheel and how much pressure would you put on the accelerator? There would be a lack of drive (so to speak), a lack of intensity, focus or energy in your actions. Where would you go? Anywhere. You're not moving forward with purpose, which means that you don't get where you want to go because you don't know where that is.

The value of having a vision is not only to get to the end 'destination', it's also about becoming a better version of you as it helps you remain focused on your purpose, your big reason 'why' as you work towards the desired outcome. Your vision will guide and help you know what is and isn't relevant to achieving the end goal when making daily decisions. It's who you and the team/business become in the process of achieving the vision that will give you an overwhelming sense of achievement.

As we discussed at the very beginning of this book, getting clear about your purpose is essential to achieving all that you want in life. It's important here to distinguish between your purpose and your vision.

Your purpose is *why* you exist. Why you're on this earth. I shared with you that my purpose is to inspire and educate people who want to learn. This is what I live by. It doesn't matter how I do this, it could be face-to-face training, through writing this book, writing and delivering an e-course or Webinar training, or simply having a conversation with a leader. Any and all of these formats for delivery assist me to achieve my purpose of inspiring and educating people who want to learn, and when I'm doing this I feel alive, I feel excited and elated. It feels like I'm on purpose.

My vision for Motivational Leadership is to 'assist leaders to develop happy people in positive work environments across the globe'. When I see happy smiling faces in workplaces across the globe, I know that my leadership training and all the hard work I've put in will have made a difference. The vision is the picture of success, what it looks like when you've achieved. As they say, a picture paints a thousand words and by achieving this vision, I know that I'll be impacting the 'happiness' of the global population.

There are two layers to your vision which you need to consider.

The **first** is your personal vision for what you want your team to achieve and what success looks like.

The **second** is the vision you want your team to help you establish, that is aligned with your own vision for your team.

In this section of the book, we will be looking at your personal vision for your team or business. Later in the book, in the Focus Section, we will look at the process of helping your team come up with the 'shared' vision for your business. What's most important at this stage is that you get clear on what your vision is, what success looks like to you.

A vision is your picture of success at a specified point in time in the future and is your reason WHY in business. It contributes to why you get out of bed in the morning. It's a picture of what success looks like, which is full of feeling, emotion, sounds and smells, anything you can add to make it as real as possible in your mind. The clearer you are on your vision, the easier it will be to achieve it. Many businesses fail because the leader fails to visualise and then communicate their vision.

What's most important about your vision at this stage is that you believe in it! Your vision will be why you do everything that you do in business. The reason behind the decisions you make, the communication you have, the discipline you assert. If you don't believe in it, then you will find it difficult to act on or make decisions in line with it and it will be a waste of the paper it's written on.

How To Establish Your Vision For Your Business/ Team:

If you take the time to do this early in your business, then you will reap the benefits down the track.

1. Know the business you are in. If you are unclear about your business, what drives it, what your key business drivers are then it will be difficult to set a vision. So make sure you know what the key business drivers are right now.
2. Set a date. When will your business have transformed into this picture?
3. Write a list of all the things you would like to see happen in your business.

Categorise them under these categories. You, Your Team, Your Customers, Your Shareholders (if relevant). Then, go crazy.

Make a list of as many things as you can think of that you would like to see happen for each category.

- How do they feel?
- What do they now get to experience?
- What is the benefit for them?
- How is their life easier or better?
- Consider how you'll improve your KBD's, your people and their performance.
- What does the achievement look like?
- Who is there celebrating with you?
- What are they saying?

4. Go ahead and start writing, don't stop – write for at least 10 minutes. You will be surprised at what comes out.

5. Now go back and re-read it. What's the main feature of this story? What do you want your one key focus to be? Pick only one. Keep it simple and easy for you and your team to remember. Edit the story until you're happy with it.

6. Come up with a 'tag line' for your vision. This is your mantra, what you say that will evoke the emotion and energy from the whole story (once you've read it to them, which we'll get to later).

This is the first stage of creating and building your vision. Most importantly, it must have meaning to you, as the leader, it must move you emotionally. If you need to add to it to evoke more emotion then do it now. Once you're clear on your vision, then all decisions you need to make in your business will become clearer, because you simply ask yourself the question, "Is this in line and will it help us achieve our vision?" If it does, then great, go ahead. If it doesn't, then forget it and refocus.

Making Profitable Decisions From The Heart

Leadership is such an important role to play in anyone's life. If you have the privilege to lead someone, then it's important to value this role and treat it with the utmost respect. Whether we are aware of it or not, being someone's leader has a great impact on their overall life experience. All you have to do is remember back to when you first began in the workforce. Who was your leader? What were they like? How did you view them? What significance did they have in your world?

It's very easy to forget the impact a leader has on their people when you become a leader, because you don't feel like you've changed. It is also easy to allow the 'status' of having a title go directly to your ego and revel in the power, rather than respecting it. You have the power to help someone really love and enjoy their job/role or to really despise coming to work and become unhappy. Who you are as a leader and the decisions you make will determine this, regardless of what the 'technical' part of the job is.

One of the biggest mistakes new leaders make is to be like the leader they are replacing. Stepping into a leadership role, especially when you are replacing a very powerful and respected leader, can be a difficult task. You have big shoes to fill. It is essential for you to remember: "You must lead as you are." Do not be like the leader you have replaced. I have done this and it DOES NOT WORK. When I did this, I felt like I was inauthentic. I couldn't remember why I was doing what I was doing, which meant all my decisions were inconsistent and I lacked integrity. Regardless of who you are replacing, be yourself and do what you think is right.

As I mentioned, Simon Sinek put it so well when he said that people think leadership credibility comes from intelligence. We established that it doesn't. It comes from your experience and willingness to learn from your mistakes. From working towards your vision, your willingness to surround yourself with more knowledgable people than yourself and your desire to help them achieve. It's also the absence of an ego and being willing to admit when you're wrong.

If you are asked a question and you don't know, then it's okay to say that. Whether you know the answer or the right decision in the moment is irrelevant; your people are looking to you for direction. The direction is your vision. As long as you are clear on your vision, then the answer is always there which ensures consistency as a leader. To make a decision from the heart, explore the possible solutions based on what your vision is, speak to people who do know and then establish your response.

So, making profitable decisions from the heart means to make decisions based on your vision. Make any decision with your vision in mind. What will move you closer to the vision? What will keep your team motivated and inspired to continue to take actions to achieve your vision? What is the best decision for your customers, so they continue to move you towards your vision? When you make decisions from this perspective, you will always be making profitable decisions in the long run.

Pain Vs Pleasure

As a leader, your role is to provide a clear way to help your team achieve what they want to achieve. Sometimes this means making the 'unpopular' decisions.

What's important to understand when you're trying to achieve your vision, is that people will do more to avoid pain than they will to gain pleasure. Most likely, without you guiding them, they will see doing the full job properly and thoroughly the first time as the painful option, because it may take longer and taking short-cuts to make their current experience 'easier' as the less painful way. Your job as the leader is to provide a disciplined environment where they know that taking the short cut is more painful, via consequences, than doing the job well and thoroughly the first time. We'll get to that later in the book. You've achieved and you know what it took to get there. Now your job is to help your team achieve all that you have, and more.

When making any decision in the business, consider your vision, the best interest of the people and the profitability of the business. Your decisions must demonstrate that you are committed to increasing the profit as well as developing your people. As long as every decision is in line with one of these factors, then you can be sure your business is on track for success.

An ugly leader is one who uses their title to make decisions based on whatever they want and feel like at the time. People lose respect very quickly for leaders who are driven by power and authority. Even if you are the business owner, it doesn't mean you can do and say whatever you want, not if you want a happy and successful team, that is. Think about a leader you've had in the past. Would they have earned your respect if they said, "Do as I say, because I'm the boss?" It's not motivating, it's not inspiring and people are certainly not going to do something just because you have a title and you said so. Would you?

As the old saying goes, "Treat people how you want to be treated." If you can say 'yes' to a request from your team member, after considering what's best for the business and for the team as a whole, then do. There is no benefit in making your team unhappy unnecessarily. It leads to low productivity and high staff turnover, giving you low profit and performance results.

So remove the need for power. As a leader, you are already powerful beyond measure, you have a huge impact on your peoples' lives. Adopt the attitude that you are now a servant to your people, your job is to help them be successful. The beauty of this is that when they are successful, then you will be successful. In fact, the degree to which your team achieves success will be to the exact degree that you achieve success. A great quote I once heard was: "The fastest way to become successful is to help others to become successful first." It's true. Help others and you'll reap the rewards ten-fold.

Feedback Is The Breakfast Of Champions

How do you see, receive and feel about mistakes and feedback you get? What do you think about making a mistake? If you are like most people, you may feel defensive or embarrassed when you make a mistake. You may hide or cover up the mistake and you may even tell a lie to avoid having to own up to making a mistake. Whether this is to your customers, your leader or your team, either way, it is a poor habit to get into. The question is, what outcome does this lead to? Most likely, if you cover it up you will make more mistakes, because you haven't learned from it, or if you're caught out lying, it can be detrimental to your business and/or your career. It leads you down a path of negativity and lack of integrity.

Now think back to the time when you were learning to walk. Well, you might not remember learning to walk yourself, however you may well know of a baby that you have observed in the process of learning to walk. Tell me, do they stand up and walk perfectly first go? I'm sure your answering with a resounding "NO". Would you expect them to get up and walk first go? Would you berate them or tell them off for not getting up and walking perfectly first go? Another resounding "NO". In fact we do the opposite, don't we? We clap and cheer and celebrate and tell them: "Well done, you can do it, give it another go!" And the more they give it a go, the more we congratulate them!

Yet, as an adult, we seem to do just the opposite of that. Sometimes we won't act if we are fearful of making a mistake. We become paralysed with fear if we've never done the 'thing' before, and if we somehow build up the courage to act and then make a mistake, we then berate ourselves for trying.

What's important to remember here is that we didn't know how to fail when we were a baby. Every able-bodied adult did not know how to fail when they were a baby. You don't see adults crawling into a room because they failed to learn to walk, do you? Have you ever seen that? Again, another resounding, "NO." Failure is learned as an adult and failure is not the same as mistakes. Go back to learning to walk. Did you, as a baby, make mistakes whilst you were learning to walk? Of course you did. You gave it a go, fell down, got back up, tweaked what you did slightly, got a little further and then fell back down again. How many times did you repeat that process? Not once, not twice, not even three or four times. It was literally hundreds or thousands of times, wasn't it?

The only way you could have failed as a baby whilst learning to walk was if you'd have given up. As adults, when we 'think' we have failed, we have a tendency to give up. The truth is, we've only failed because we have 'given up'. If we chose to see a mistake, or getting something wrong, as simply 'feedback' on how not to do it next time and continue after tweaking our actions, do you think that would have an impact on how successful we became?

So, the challenge, if you choose to accept it, is to redefine what 'making a mistake' means to you. If you choose to see it as an opportunity to get better at something, how do you think you would feel about mistakes? If you choose to see it as feedback on how not to do it next time and learn from it, then you will feel more confident to give it another go.

You will allow yourself to go for something that you're not sure of or haven't done before, because it is okay to get it wrong. I've often heard quotes of highly successful entrepreneurs saying something like, "I've just failed more times than everyone else." Life isn't a dress rehearsal and staying safe and stuck in your comfort zone NEVER gives you a sense of satisfaction, reward or achievement. You only get one go at this life, so make it okay to make mistakes, forgive yourself and allow yourself the opportunity that every human being *should* have, to give it a go and be okay with getting it wrong. It has no bearing on who you are as a person. In fact, the only thing that has a bearing on who you are as a person is whether or not you are willing to step outside of your comfort zone to give something a go. That will determine who you are as a person much faster than any 'mass' of mistakes you could think of.

Remember this: *The faster you make the mistakes, the faster you will become successful.*

As a leader, once you can view mistakes like this then it's important that you help your team to see them in the same way. It must be okay for your team to learn and make mistakes too.

Remember a time when your parents tried to tell you that doing something was a mistake, and if you'd only listen to them then you wouldn't have to go through the pain of learning it the hard way. I remember my parents allowing me to make my own mistakes. They could quite clearly see that the decisions I was making were not the right ones, however they also knew that telling me so would have made me even more determined to do it my way. The best example that comes to mind is when I got married at 23 years of age. They wondered how this marriage would work, how we would raise children together as we were two very different individuals. However, they still handed over the cash for the wedding, watched as we said our vows and celebrated. When I approached them 16 months later and said, "This isn't working, I'm leaving," my parents said, "Yes, we wondered how you would make that marriage work."

Now let me tell you what would have happened if they had said to me, "Don't marry him, he's not right for you." It would have made me all the more determined and probably out of stubbornness, I would have stayed with him for a lot longer than I did, causing even more unhappiness for everyone.

As it turned out, I learned more about what I did and didn't need in a partner and, more importantly, I learned more about me. This relationship was important in my growth and development as an adult, and he is a very special person that I'm eternally grateful to. We are still friends to this day.

So the key to this story is that just like a parent, sometimes as a leader you must let your people make mistakes, even if you think you know better. Your telling them will have little or no impact on their learning and development, which is what your job is as a leader. As long as they are not in physical harm or danger, then often the best way to help them learn is to let them make their own mistakes. This can be very difficult and does require a lot of patience. It is for that reason that you MUST have the clear expectations implemented into your business, as they help to minimise the risk.

There is a great model of questioning to help you embrace this mindset. It will help you remain calm, open and accepting of their mistakes. If you commit to always asking these four questions, when a mistake occurs, your team member's confidence and growth will happen much faster. So when a mistake happens, ask:

1. What happened?
2. What have you learned?

3. What are you going to change to ensure that it doesn't happen again?

4. How would you like me to hold you accountable should this happen again?

There is a great story that comes from a senior executive at IBM. An employee sheepishly walked into his office after having made a mistake that cost the company one million dollars. He handed his boss an envelope, which contained his resignation letter.

The boss said, "What is this?"

The employee replied, "It's my resignation letter, I understand that I've just made a huge mistake and am not wanted on the team anymore."

To that, the boss replied, "I absolutely will not accept your resignation. Why would I accept your resignation when I've just invested one million dollars into your education? Now, get back to work."

With a huge sigh of relief and a smile on his face, the employee resumed his work.

The better you become at keeping frustration out of these conversations and replacing it with empathy and understanding, the more confident and successful your team will be. You can find empathy and understanding through the fact that *if you had the exact same experiences, beliefs and perceptions as this person, then you too would have made exactly the same mistake*.

> To stretch your thinking just a little more go to www.leadershipskillsreducethebills. com and down load your article "All Beliefs Are Based On Lies" with my compliments.

PART 2
Communication

Chapter 4: Defining Communication

"Communication is a skill that you can learn. It's like riding a bicycle or typing. If you're willing to work at it, you can rapidly improve the quality of every part of your life."

~ Brian Tracy

Whilst being clear on who you are as a leader is important, how you communicate will demonstrate who you are, without you even being aware of it. So it's crucial that we take a deep look at what communication is and how we can construct our communication for a positive outcome. The clearer we communicate as leaders, with well-thought-out plans, the more responsive and positive our people will remain. When you communicate in advance, you're ahead of the eight ball. This comes from having a clear intention and being organised, which we'll discuss in detail, and it's where your strength and power will come from as a leader. It's also important to understand the power of communication within relationships. If you have a tendency to put your relationships before your leadership, then you may be undoing all the positivity that you've built up until now. In this chapter, we'll explore:

- What is communication?

- How to communicate clear expectations with consequences.
- Your leadership vs your friendships and how to prioritise them.

This chapter is all about building the foundation of your understanding of communication. Because when you know what you're working with and what's possible, you can achieve almost anything.

What Is Communication?

Communication determines the quality of our experience of the outside world, affecting both how we communicate with others and how we receive communication.

> *The quality of our communication can be*
> *determined by the response that we get.*

If we don't like the way someone responds to us, it's our responsibility as a leader to change the way we communicate to obtain a response that we are looking for. I get this is a large statement to digest and can be difficult to swallow. After all, it's not up to you to determine how someone responds to you. I totally get it. However, remove any objection for a minute and try it on. What if you were able to determine how someone responds to you simply by tailoring your communication to the intended person? Imagine how that would impact your business, your results and even your career.

Not everyone will embrace this idea, and they will therefore carry on with average communication skills. If, however, you're committed to improving your leadership and the results you get, then this concept deserves some consideration. Understanding this and applying it requires a willingness on your part, as the leader, to take complete responsibility for your communication.

If and when you do, you will have greater relationships with your people and achieve far superior results.

Great quality communication is the key to leading a team successfully because when you communicate effectively, you will give yourself a greater opportunity to achieve your goals through helping others achieve theirs. You can help others improve when under-performing, resolve conflict more efficiently, deal with customer complaints easily and engage your people in your vision in a powerful way, ultimately enabling you to run a more successful and profitable business.

The Oxford definition of communication is, "the imparting or exchanging of information by speaking, writing, or using some other medium." It's important to understand that our communication is not just the words we speak. In fact, words are the smallest component of communication and if you limit your understanding to just the words you speak, then you are limiting the impact you can have with your communication. The words you use when speaking equate to only 7% of the communication that the receiver hears from you. In saying that, take a moment to review the towards vs away language under the focus section in chapter two. The words you choose are still important when communicating as a leader.

When selecting the words you use, it's important to consider your intention for the communication. The following table explains how to construct your message for the greatest impact as well as how to gauge the quality of your communication based on the response you get.

Construct the message	Think about your desired outcome – set your intention.
	How do you want this person to walk away feeling?
	What do you want them to think about and focus on?
Form of Communication	Will it be talking face-to-face, over the phone, via email or in a written note? *See rule at the end of this section.
Deconstruct the message	Each person will hear different messages from the same communication, so it's important that you are clear. A good way to manage this is to ask them to repeat back to you what they have heard.
Receiver	When the receiver gives the communicator feedback in the form of response, this determines the quality of the communication.

Based on this model, if you get a response from the receiver that you don't like or weren't expecting, then take a moment to reflect on what your intention was and how you believe you communicated it. It's also important to look at how you communicated what you said, in the context of your tonality and body language. Once you've done that, review what you could change and recompose how you will communicate using your tonality, body language and by rephrasing your words.

'Tonality' means the level of excitement or level of misery in your voice. Think about if you were to say, "I'm so excited!" in a dull voice or "I'm really sad," in an excited voice. It can be quite difficult to formulate and may take some practice. Ask people around you what they hear when you say these statements in the said tonality.

Tonality contributes a massive 38% of your communication and is the tone, pitch and inflection you use in your sentence. There are three types of tonality that we communicate with: **Question, Statement** and **Command** tonality.

A question tonality can have any level of tonality throughout the statement and finishes the last syllable of the last word with a higher pitch, which sounds like you are asking a question. This implies uncertainty or lack of knowledge around the subject being spoken about.

The most well-known example to demonstrate the 'Question Tonality' is from the movie *American Pie* where the teenage girl is talking and she says "And there was this one time, at band camp..." "And there was this one time, at band camp..." over and over again, where she finishes her sentence on a high note. Think about your perception of this girl. What, in your opinion, is her intelligence level? How much credibility does she have? Would you trust her with your life or, for that matter, your money? It's easy to see that she lacks credibility, she doesn't sound very intelligent and I don't know about you, but I certainly wouldn't trust her with any large sums of money, much less my life.

Imagine you were to hear a surgeon ask a nurse, "Can you pass me the scalpel?", or a police officer say, "Can you please take a deep breath, and blow into the bag?" or the bouncer of a club say, "Excuse me. You've had enough to drink, can you please leave?" finishing on a high note with each example. You would struggle to respect him/her and do as they say, wouldn't you?

As a leader, there is little or no use for the question tonality. You are the leader, so your people are looking to you for certainty and direction. If using 'question tonality' is a habit, know that simply having the awareness of this will help you change it. Listen to yourself when you speak and if you hear it, just re-articulate what you've said with command tonality. It will feel a little uncomfortable to begin with, but the more you practise it, and acknowledge it, the more familiar command tonality will become.

A statement tonality, is talking in a 'mono' tone. The same tone for the whole sentence or statement. It can appear quite lacklustre and inspires nothing from the receiver.

It can be quite 'boring' to listen to and no matter what is said, the tone is constant for the whole sentence. They could be saying, "Congratulations, that's brilliant news," but if it's monotone, then you would hear the tone before you hear the words.

As a leader, if you constantly speak with a monotone, you will find it difficult to inspire and motivate your team. Selling the vision will be extremely difficult in a mono tonality. Now you have awareness of it, begin to practice using some inflection in your voice when something is exciting or you're happy about something. Adopt the command tonality to demonstrate knowledge and authority in your voice, giving you more credibility as a leader.

Command tonality is exactly that, it sounds like a command. It is when you speak with any amount of inflection and tone throughout the sentence and then finish the final syllable of the last word in the sentence on a low note, or deeper than the rest of the sentence. This implies certainty, knowledge and clarity around what is being spoken. It communicates a sense of authority, regardless of whether the communicator has authority or not. Using this technique gives the person a sense of credibility. They appear to know what they are talking about.

Think of the same surgeon speaking in an authoritative tone, "Can you pass me the scalpel?" finishing the last syllable of the word 'scalpel' in a lower tone than the rest of the sentence. Or, "Can you please take a deep breath, and blow into the bag?" or the bouncer patting you on the shoulder, saying "Excuse me, you've had enough to drink, can you please leave?" Even if the communicator is a little nervous, the mere fact that they speak with command tonality, finishing the last syllable of the sentence on a lower note, would give them a presence of authority and they would sound credible. The receiver would also be more likely to believe they have authority as they appear confident, which makes this a great "fake it 'til you make it" tool.

If you currently speak with command tonality, then there is no need to change, as this will help you communicate clear directions and your people will feel safe with you leading the way.

If you are unclear about which tonality you habitually use, then explain this to a friend and ask them to give you feedback. It must be when you're not thinking about it, so share it and then forget it and carry on. You may find their observations interesting.

The third form of communication is that of body language. Body language is comprised of, but not limited to, your posture, the position of your arms, your legs, facial expressions, the direction of your body, and how you hold yourself. Body language forms a whopping 55% of your entire communication when speaking to someone face-to-face.

I remember one of my team members in my first store shared with me that when they approached me to ask me a question, sometimes I looked at them like I was disgusted with them. When they told me this, I remember being extremely surprised and taken back by this feedback, as it was never my intention to look at them like that.

As a result, we established that it may have been when I was feeling under pressure, so I invited them to ask the question, "Have you got a moment for me to ask a question?" which then gave me the opportunity to check in with my facial expression, and say "Yes, of course," or, "Give me a moment."

If your arms and legs are crossed, or you're facing away from the 'receiver' and have a tight or stressed look on your face, then your body language is closed. You're communicating that you are unapproachable, disinterested, not open to others and people will not feel that they can approach you for help.

If your arms and legs are uncrossed and your posture is straight, you have a smile or relaxed look on your face and the direction of your body is towards them, then people will feel that they can approach you for help and feel comfortable in your presence.

*Number 1 Rule for E-mail communication:

Never communicate bad news in an email. Because the receiver cannot ascertain tonality or body language in an email. It's very difficult to articulate clearly and exactly what the news is without people drawing their own conclusion and beginning to fret about the meaning or impact of this news. This can cause unnecessary disharmony to a team. All bad news must be communicated in person with a well-thought-out plan of how you will deliver it. This way, as a leader, you can manage fear, answer questions and help return the group back to harmony as soon as possible.

Communicating Clear Expectations and Consequences

There is a model founded by Anthony Robins called the 'six core needs'. We will go into more detail about this in Part 4: Environment, but it's necessary to mention here to help you understand the impact of clear expectations vs no expectations. One of humanity's basic core needs is that of certainty, which can also be generalised as safety. To help humans to achieve a level of comfort in life, it's important that they experience a degree of certainty and safety. Safety can be described as knowing you have a roof over your head at night, knowing where your next meal is coming from, and knowing that the people around you will treat you with love and respect. In the work environment, safety and certainty are met by being clear on what is expected of you and knowing how to complete the tasks required.

Now let me ask you, have you ever worked in an environment where you didn't know what was expected of you? Have you ever experienced 'moving goal posts', where you thought you were doing the right thing, only to find out that expectations have changed again and have not been communicated to you? Have you ever been reprimanded for something that you weren't aware of? If you have, then you'll know exactly what I'm talking about. If you haven't, then imagine for a moment what it would be like to work in an environment as described above. It would be extremely unpleasant and very difficult, if not impossible, to be successful, as you are simply focused on surviving the day, rather than trying to achieve any level of success.

These are all symptoms of a leader not setting clear expectations. Clear expectations are one of the most important things a leader can communicate, because when your team members are clear and understand what is expected of them, they can then focus on achieving instead of merely surviving, are more likely to do their job, do it well, have discipline, and be happy in the workplace.

So, as a leader, why do you think it's important to set clear expectations? I'm sure some of my teams in the past have thought that I set expectations just to annoy them, just to make their life difficult. This isn't the case at all. The only reason I will have an expectation in my business is to help them and the business get the greatest possible outcome/result. That's it.

Clear expectations are exactly that. Documented expectations of what must happen in the business. They are not an "It would be nice if..." or, "When you feel like..." scenario. They are "What *must* happen." This is from simple things such as what it means to be on time to what it sounds like to answer the phone correctly.

The easiest and best way to set clear expectations is this:

If there is something that happens that is frustrating for the customers or causing customer complaints – set an expectation.

If there is something that happens that is frustrating for you as the leader – set an expectation.

If there is something that happens that is frustrating for the whole team – set an expectation.

Make a list of all things that fall under one of the 3 categories above, in addition to already existing expectations of the business that have a purpose and lead to a desired outcome. The best way to set these expectations in the beginning is with the team. The more ownership they have on these expectations, the more likely they are to uphold them. It will also make your life much easier down the track when you need to hold them accountable to the expectations. It can be done over a series of meetings under different subjects to ensure it's all covered and your people are not overloaded in one sitting.

Then, to ensure that it is clear, you must document these expectations. This gives you something to reference when this 'frustrating' thing happens in the future. Whilst conducting the meeting, ensure someone is typing up the agreed expectations so it's able to be printed, signed by the team and posted up somewhere where the staff will see it. Then when you have a new team member join, you can simply give them a copy of the list at their orientation, have them read through it and come back to you if they have any questions. This keeps the whole team on the same page – it's clear communication. It's a step towards helping your team focus on success rather than just survival.

This is the first step when creating your structure, because you will build the rest of your structure around these expectations. So hold this meeting first, before a vision or business planning meeting.

Once you have documented your expectations as a team, this becomes a working document that you can update and add to in the event that something goes wrong and you need to add another expectation. Just make sure you communicate it clearly also.

Now, just having documented expectations isn't enough. It's a natural tendency for humans to seek out the shortest and easiest route to the end. Even if it means not getting the results or outcome they want. As long as they can get to the end (whatever they perceive that to be) the easiest way with the least amount of hard work or sweat, that is what most people will search for.

This is because human beings will do more to avoid pain than they will to gain pleasure. The problem is that this thinking is all for the 'now' based thinking, all for the present. There is no long-term thinking, no consideration of consequences down the track and, more often than not, it turns out to be more painful in the long run. They just haven't thought it through clearly enough.

A great example of this is exercising. Think about it. When you embark on a fitness regime, you're motivated because something has happened. Maybe your clothes are too tight, you can't wear your favourite jeans, or someone says something to you. Whatever it is, it seems less painful to get out of bed in the morning than it does dealing with clothes not fitting or people making comments. So you exercise for 3 or 4 days, and you're feeling good.

Then, you have a late night, you're working like crazy and the alarm goes off at 6am for you to get up and exercise. It's winter and it's freezing outside. You lay there and justify why you don't have to do it this morning "I've been good, I've done it four times this week. I'll do it tonight. I'm tired. I've been working hard." At 6.00 in the morning, it's less painful to 'justify' and stay in bed, than it is to get out of bed to exercise.

Unless...

You fast forward your life 10 years, to where you have done this justification of not getting out of bed, day in day out, for 10 years. Then you've justified why you can't in the evening. Before you know it, you've put on 50kg and you can barely walk with comfort, let alone do any sort of solid exercise. You can no longer fit into any nice clothes, and you now have to settle for anything that fits. You feel unhealthy, you lack energy, you almost look grey, and people are asking you with genuine concern if you're okay.

Now, as you lay in bed in the morning, which one seems the least painful? Based on the picture described, staying in bed seems more painful, doesn't it? So, as a leader, you must recreate a similar scenario, in relation to work, with varying degrees of consequences.

This is why you must implement consequences. This is one thing many leaders struggle to implement effectively, because enforcing the consequence can be seen as a confrontational conversation/action or experience, and it seems that it would be easier to just not acknowledge it (which is the leader taking the easiest, shortest, least-amount-of-work route). Seems like it would be the easiest way to go. But wait, is it?

Fast forward 2 years. The leader of the business has had clear expectations in place, but no one has listened or adhered to them and the leader hasn't enforced them. The customers are frustrated because no one gets back to them and no one seems to care about them. The team is frustrated because why should they do it, if no one else will. They will do as little as possible, because there's no consequence. The atmosphere is shot, there is no fun, everyone feels stressed because they don't know what is expected of them as the expectations aren't followed or discussed. There is pressure to achieve with no support, no one feels appreciated, and the team is barely a team. They can't wait for finish time so they can go home!

Have you ever heard of such an environment?

This all started because there were either no expectations, or no consequences for not doing the minimum expectations.

Now, which one sounds easier, what has just been described or having the 'tough' conversation to address under-performance? As the leader, the choice is yours. To be a motivational leader, you must be disciplined with your expectations and follow through with consequences. Later in the book, I explain a structure to help you have this 'tough' conversation so it's clear and easy, with no emotion attached.

Deciding on the consequence is specific to the business you're in. The 'consequence' must represent the severity of the 'offence'. It's no good having a severe consequence for a minor breach of the expectations, especially for the first time.

Often the consequence can simply be the 'severe' conversation that you have with them articulating the seriousness of the breach with your language and tone, keeping in mind your intention, what you want them to walk away knowing, thinking and feeling.

Other suggested minor consequences can be cleaning out the kitchen fridge, if you have one; buying the team coffee; cleaning up an area of the working environment. Most importantly, you must ensure that the consequence fits the offence. You will know if it does when you think about enforcing it.

Remember, this also applies to you. If you don't meet expectations, you must also experience the consequence. That's when the 'lead by example' rubber hits the road.

Leadership vs Friendship

If you are friends with any of your team members or become a leader of the team that you have worked with previously as colleagues, it can be challenging to establish yourself as a leader, because they know you as a person and what you are like when you haven't got a 'vested' interest in the business. There can be many pot holes at this point and if you have some knowhow at the very beginning, it can make your life a lot easier in the long run.

What's important to remember is that when you become a leader, you must reevaluate your priorities, because friendship can no longer be at the top of your list. Quality leadership must become more important than being friends with your team, if you want to achieve success as a leader. Your team members have enough friends, what they need is a leader. Someone who will make the tough decisions, the right decisions for the business to assist the whole team to progress, not just the popular decisions. When you do reprioritise, then and only then will you begin to earn the respect of your team, which is important because your team don't *have* to do anything you say, they don't *have* to respect you. Whilst you can always 'get rid of them' eventually, until you learn this, you will be deemed to repeat the same experience until you learn the lesson that leadership and respect must be earned. I've seen it time and time again, where as soon as someone gains the title of 'Leader', they think that the team should automatically respect them and do whatever they say. I'm sorry to be the bearer of bad news, but it's not going to happen.

Who says they have to respect you and who's going to make them? Leadership is an earned position, as is respect, and you do this by prioritising your leadership over the friendships you have with your team. Just because you have the title, doesn't mean anything to them. You must earn it, like everyone else has. You can either learn this now, or learn it the hard way. Let me tell you, the hard way is very painful and pretty much includes a full staff turnover, so you can start fresh with the new team where you earn their respect as a leader. So if you don't want to retrain a whole new team, then apply this now so you don't have to go through a full staff turnover.

As a friend and when you're amongst a group of friends, you may potentially do what is the popular or accepted thing. You may even say what you think your friends think, and agree with them, most of all, you want to be accepted as a person and belong to your group of friends. Whether you do this on purpose or whether it happens naturally, because you've selected friends similar to yourself, is irrelevant. The point is that there is a reason why you have the friends you do, you have similar views or interests.

Unfortunately or fortunately, depending on where you're coming from, leadership is almost the opposite of this. As a leader, more often than not you need to make unpopular decisions. You must consider what is best for the business as well as the people and deliver that in a way they can understand, even if they don't like it. Your people already have a set of friends, they don't need another friend. They need a leader.

Often what people want and what is best for them are two different things. As we discussed in the last chapter, most people want to take the shortest, easiest route, not the well thought out route. Being a leader is about helping them choose the well thought out route, which will lead them to them to greater success than if they were to continue to take the short cut. Leadership is about respecting and gaining respect rather than just being liked. You gain respect firstly by respecting your people and then by helping them achieve success.

There are some big red flags that are good to be clear on from the day you begin as their leader, which will make your life a whole lot easier in the long run.

Title behaviour – the greatest way to lose respect is to behave on your title. Have you ever had a leader like this? They say 'no' just because they can. They have a "Do as I say not as I do" approach. They think, *Now I am the leader, I can do whatever I like and they must do as I say*. They disrespect the team, not caring for the people because they see themselves as more superior now and don't need them to progress. They use their position as power, doing all of the above, saying 'no' for the thrill of it, not explaining 'why' if they have to say no, and doing things that they wouldn't allow their team to get away with. They don't do things that the team members are expected to do, seeing them as a numbers/certain output rather than human beings who have feelings, a family and friends, and a life outside of work.

A great mentor of mine, my dad, always taught me to 'Save 'no' for the big things'. The best way to get the most out of your people is to say 'yes' when you can. If you can say 'yes' then do. But ensure that you think through the impact saying 'yes' will have on your business, the rest of the team and your customers. Always do the quick check when asked a question like, "Can I leave early/have this day off?"

1.   What's best for the business?
2.   What's best for the team?
3.   What's best for the customers?

Then, if after doing this quick check there is a valid and clear reason why you can't say 'yes', and you tried every which way to make it a 'yes', then explain it to them with, "No, unfortunately we can't this time because…" Always offer a reason why you can't and ensure they understand. "Because I said so," isn't a good enough answer, if you want them to respect and accept your decision.

If you can't think through the checklist and consequences of the decision clearly on the spot, then say, "Can I think about it and get back to you?" Then you can write it out, so you can see it visually to help you think through the process in the beginning. The purpose is to ensure that you don't allow a friendship or familiarity with your people to cloud your vision for the business and the team. Remain on purpose by following your vision and if you can say 'yes', then do. You will earn more respect and gain greater results from them in the long run if you do. After all, every relationship is based on give and take.

Chapter 5:
Building Your Tool Box

*"If you only have a hammer, you tend to
see every problem as a nail."*

~ Abraham Maslow

The way you value your people is demonstrated clearly in your communication. As a leader and as a business, it's important to understand that your most valuable asset is your people. The quality of the people you attract to your business will have a great impact on the results of your bottom line. This is quite simply determined by how you value your people. If you place little importance and value on your people and what they experience in your working environment, then you are unlikely to retain people for any long-term period. If you understand the value of your people, then that will be conveyed in your communication and your behaviour, and your people will be more likely to stay for the long-term. One of the best ways to value your people is to ensure that you always have a clear intention for what you're communicating. If you don't know the direction of your communication, then you're waffling and people will just switch off. Either that or your communication may come across as offensive on some level.

Like in any relationship, it's also important to understand the power of your appreciation and trust, when looking to demonstrate the value you place on people.

In this chapter, we're going to explore:

- How to set a clear intention.
- How to earn trust.
- Understanding the power of appreciation.
- Understanding the emotional credit or debt equation.

Once we have explored this, we'll be ready to have some extremely powerful conversations.

Setting A Clear Intention

Imagine there are two people making up a story that isn't true and sharing it with a group of people. The first person's intention is to help this group achieve all they want to achieve. The second person's intention is to rip them off to benefit him/herself. The first person is called 'a story teller', whereas the second person is known as 'a liar'.

I remember when I was studying coaching and the mind, a key lesson that stuck with me, was that if you know what you want, your brain will go out searching for that result. If you don't know what you want or you only know what you don't want, then you could get anything. However, one thing is certain: you won't get what you *do* want. When I was coaching, I would go into each coaching session with an intention in mind. Usually it was to simply serve the client to get their desired outcome. In doing this, I removed me and my agenda, and was simply present for the client.

Your behaviour as a leader is important. However, your intention behind that behaviour is even more important. What you intend to achieve out of your communication or behaviour will ultimately determine what you communicate. So it's important that, as a leader, whatever you do, know what your desired outcome is, so you can figure out how you're going to get there.

Everything human beings do, whether aware of it or not, begins with an intention. To scratch your little toe, to go to the fridge for some food, to brush your teeth, everything happens because first we had an intention to do so. Whether we are aware of the intention or not is irrelevant.

Why is this important? Well, when you are communicating, interacting and ultimately leading a team, you have an intention that is driving you. Your intention will be the very thing that determines how you behave and therefore your outcome. So it's important to be consciously aware of exactly what your intention is so that you can choose your behaviour, which will determine what your outcome will be. This can be from something as small as one conversation with a team member, to something as big as achieving your yearly goal.

Intention is simply 'a thing intended, an aim, or a plan', according to the Oxford Dictionary. More specifically, it is being clear on what you would like the outcome to be of any situation, conversation or one year goal. Setting your intention is quite simple if you follow these 4 steps:

1. Get clear on exactly what outcome you are looking for and write it down.
2. State what it is you would like the outcome to be to someone else, or at least out loud.
3. Take the first step towards achieving this outcome.
4. Acknowledge yourself for taking the action and identify the next step.

As I have already alluded, this can be applied in a variety of contexts. From something as small and simple as a conversation, to something as big as the vision and yearly goal you are going for. So, as a leader, it's not just your behaviour that matters; it's your intention behind the behaviour that will determine your results.

I remember when I first started as a leader and something went wrong, or one of my team members made a mistake which led to a customer complaint. I would feel frustrated, especially if it was an experienced team member. I know it sounds bad, but I would have this innate desire to make sure they felt bad for what they'd done and know that it was wrong. It seems quite nasty, I know. I think that was me being self-righteous, where I just wanted them to know that they had done wrong.

But then I'd take a moment and think about the desired outcome and I knew that if I made them feel bad and wrong, then the only thing I'd achieve would be to demoralise them, putting a dint in their self-confidence and making them upset with me, therefore reducing their productivity.

So, I'd get clear on what my intention for the communication was and then approach the situation from that perspective. For example: *My intention is to help my team member understand what has happened, what behaviour led to this outcome and help them choose a new strategy in the future.* Needless to say, they would walk away knowing what they needed to do and how to do it. Most importantly, they walked away feeling positive and empowered to improve, rather than negative and devalued.

ACTIVITY:

It is for that reason that I strongly recommend getting clear on what your intention is as a leader. What is your overriding intention that you operate from on a daily basis? This is usually closely related to your purpose; it's what drives you and determines your communication and actions. My intention was to help my team be as successful as possible. Having a clear intention helped me by guiding the way I communicated with my team and determined what I did in my business. Here are some suggestions of 'intentions' that some leaders have chosen in the past to get the juices flowing:

- To make a difference in people's lives.
- To be as successful as possible by helping all of those around me become successful.
- To help people achieve.
- To win at all costs – Then get out of leadership and get into sales!

What is your overriding intention as a leader?

_____

_____

_____

When you are clear on your intention as a leader, it will guide you through all circumstances and assist you to achieve your goal.

A 'Customer Complaint' Case Study:

Despite being twice shown how to do a certain task correctly, a team member has repeated the same mistake, this time resulting in a customer complaint. This is going to cost the business money to fix the problem for the customer. It can be frustrating as a leader to have this situation occur. However if you communicate with them in the wrong tone, asking them, "Why did you do that?" or "Why didn't you read your notes?" What is that team member going to walk away thinking and feeling? They would feel bad, angry with themselves, frustrated, not good enough for the job, and their confidence and self-esteem would drop. Now, lets go back to the 'be, do, have' model. What are the qualities and emotions of a successful team member on a daily basis? Feeling good, happy with self, content, successful and a healthy confidence about themselves is when they will be their most successful. So my question to you is, "Is showing that level of frustration and anger worth it? Because it will most likely cost you a few hundred dollars in productivity for the day or worse, a few thousand for the week or month."

So we must get clear on what our desired outcome is at the end of the conversation, so we know how we must communicate to achieve that outcome. As we've explored, the simple steps in any communication are as follows:

1. Think about what you want the team member to walk away thinking and feeling.
2. Tailor your conversation and tonality to match that desired outcome.

For example:

I want the team member to walk away feeling empowered and focused ready to step up, having learned from this mistake.

This is the conversation I would have:

"So, Jake, tell me about your decision to do _____."

"As you reflect on that decision, what does hindsight tell you?"

"Okay, so what have you learned from this situation?"

"How are you going to change what you do in this situation so this never happens again?"

"Is there anything I can do to help you cement what you've learned?"

"Can I give you some feedback/suggestions on how to improve what you do?"

"Awesome, so as long as you don't make this mistake again, it's been a great investment. If it does happen again, you'll be letting me know that you haven't taken the care to learn from this."

"How are you going with your goals today, are you on track, do you need to refocus?" From this example, can you see how they will be able to move on and refocus a lot quicker than if they were 'told off' and in trouble.

Catch your people out doing the right thing, and reward them more than you would reprimand them for doing the wrong thing!

INTENTION AND COMMUNICATION:

The great thing about understanding the concept of 'intention' is that it can help you when dealing with tough situations like conflict between team members, individual issues of team members, and even issues between yourself and employees. The foundation to each of these situations that helps determine a positive result fairly seamlessly is being clear on the initial intention. When setting an intention for any form of communication, follow these 4 steps:

1. Get clear on exactly what outcome you are looking for and communicate it.
2. Ask the receiver of your communication what their desired outcome is.
3. Establish where you're at now (this helps you identify the gap).
4. Work towards closing the gap.

INTENTION AND CUSTOMER COMPLAINTS:

When you are having a conversation with a customer because they are unhappy about something, if you interrupt, answer back or appear uninterested in what they want, how is that conversation going to go? It's pretty clear, you're going to add fuel to the fire and pretty soon the complaint will be about you and not what they were initially concerned about.

If you were to set your intention before the conversation and then ask the customer at the beginning what their desired outcome was, you would have a much better chance to achieving that desired outcome.

The best way to do this with a customer complaint is to simply ask the question, "Okay, so what would you like the outcome to be from this conversation?" The key to this is to not respond with a 'yes' or a 'no' at this point in time, but simply to say, "Okay, so tell me where are we at now?"

How to manage a customer complaint with intention:

1. Communicate your intention (e.g. To help resolve their current concern or issue).
2. Ask what the desired outcome is for the customer.
3. Respond only with "Okay, so tell me, where are we at now?"

By asking these questions, you have identified the gap. You know where they are now and what the desired outcome is, so now you can simply help them by closing the gap. Your customer must always feel like you are on their side. It's you and them against the problem – ALWAYS!!!

INTENTION AND SALES:

Another example of this is with sales. If you're in a retail environment, imagine if every team member in your store set the intention to 'get the sale' for every single customer who called or walked through the door! Tell me, how would their behaviour, or more to the point, their communication, differ from what it currently is?

What we decide the customer is, or what the outcome will be before we communicate with them, will more than likely determine the outcome. Even if the customer had decided they were going to buy before they walked through the door, our behaviour/customer service will still determine whether that eventuates. So the key to this is to ensure that you and your team are ALWAYS providing customer service with the intention of getting the sale. That way you have the best opportunity to make your time as productive as possible!

Earning Trust

Have you ever experienced a relationship that is rock solid and you could trust that person with your life? How do you feel about that relationship? How do you feel about the person? It's like it's a certainty, a knowledge that no matter what, that person will always be there for you, through good times and bad. You have a deeper connection with them than most other people and you would most probably do anything for them too.

Have you ever been in a relationship or had a friend who you cannot trust? Have you ever had a leader or a teacher who would fly off the handle for no apparent reason, or have you ever confided in someone only to have them betray you? How do you feel about that person? How do you feel about the relationship? It's uncertain, isn't it? There's little safety with this person and not a great deal of connection. How far would you stretch yourself for this person? If you're like most people, you wouldn't do any more than the required bare minimum for them.

Trust is one of the key foundations in any relationship, whether it be friends, partner, teacher or leader. We are all humans and we all have feelings that need to be nurtured. If we can trust our leader, then we are more likely to open up and share what's really going on, what's preventing us from taking action, from improving our output. We are also more likely to go above and beyond for them, give ten percent more and push ourselves a little harder.

As a leader, you need your team to help you achieve success. You can't do it on your own. Your willingness alone is not enough. You are only one part of the equation, you need the other part of the equation to be successful. The other part of the equation is your team and their willingness to share the truth, to open up and be vulnerable in the hope that you will help them. No matter how good you are, if you don't earn the trust of your people, you will struggle to achieve your greatest goals.

The definition of trust is: "A firm belief in the reliability, truth, or ability of someone or something." Let's break down that definition:

A firm belief	– means there is no question in their mind.
Reliability	– A leader must be consistent in their behaviour. For example: they will do what they say they will do, they will behave in a consistent manner and will not have emotional swings of anger or frustration.
Truth	– A leader will always be honest regardless of the consequence. For example: the leader won't lie to make the team member feel better or worse.
Ability	– The leader is competent enough to help the individual achieve and progress as they desire.

Sometimes we feel like we need to defend ourselves. It's no different for leaders. It may be that a team member has suggested that the leader hasn't done their job properly, or a customer attacks them or a team member. What's important to understand when something like this happens is that you will gain nothing from becoming angry or defensive.

Remember what we explored in "Intention". What do you want the outcome to be from this conversation? It's not what your team member or customer is saying that determines who you are as a leader, it's your response. Their opinion is just that – their opinion – you are a leader for a reason. There is no need to be egotistical and prove it over and over again with assertion and defensiveness.

When someone attacks you or you feel you must defend, then seek information to understand.

1. What has led them to say what they are saying?
2. Why they are saying it and how it impacts them.
3. What their desired outcome is.

If your team members feel that you are approachable and they can tell you what they feel without you flying off the handle, then you are more likely to have a successful team.

I remember early on in my leadership career, I had a team member who was angry at me because my mother-in-law washed my clothes (I'm not that domestic). How this was relevant in the workplace, I am yet to figure out, however, I knew that my reaction was imperative. If I reacted with anger and shock and a 'how dare you' response, how do you think the conversation would have ended? How do you think that person would feel? What level of productivity do you think they would achieve for days, and possibly even weeks, afterwards?

I knew my leadership at work wasn't determined by whether or not I did my washing at home. So I simply responded with, "That's interesting, why is this an issue for you? Tell me how this impacts you at work?"

What would you like to achieve from having this conversation?

I adopted the attitude that I was not a porcelain doll and I wasn't going to shatter if they said something I didn't like. It may appear at first glance that this is allowing your people to walk all over you like a door mat. However, it's the opposite because if you don't know what they are thinking and how they are feeling, you can't do anything about it. It's better they tell you so you can do something about it – in this case, help them see reason – rather than bottle it up and it diminish their productivity.

If you adopt this attitude, it will make them feel empowered and in return they will trust you, which means you have a greater chance of success through their success. You can always walk away and scream into a pillow at a later date. This was one of the many times I did that!

So the keys to trust are:

- Invite any and all feedback.
- Know your intention (desired outcome).
- Select behaviour that demonstrates that intention (which leads to the desired outcome).
- Be unwavering in that behaviour, no matter what happens or is said.
- Be curious and ask questions to find out what the problem is, if there is one.
- Do what you say you will do, ALWAYS follow through.
- Be consistent with everything, especially your emotions.

The Power Of Appreciation

Can you remember a time when you've been really proud of completing a project, whether it was at work or home? You'd spent a long time preparing for it, working on it, and finally you completed it with a positive outcome. Your partner or leader approached you and was genuinely delighted for you and with your work. Their reaction was almost overwhelming. They were so full of enthusiasm and appreciation for your hard work. How did you feel about the completion of the project, compared with before their reaction? How did you feel about yourself? Isn't it true that your feeling of achievement and confidence increases as you are appreciated? If another person came in and responded in the same way, your positivity and confidence levels would be sky high.

Have you ever worked really hard on something and been really proud of it, only for no body to recognise it or say 'thank you'? Have you ever given your all, more than what's expected, for it to go unnoticed? How does it make you feel when this happens? Doesn't it mean the next time you're asked to do something or work on a project, you will do just that little bit less? When that goes unappreciated then the next time, you'll do a little bit less again until you get to the point where you don't take any care or pride in your work, because regardless of whether you do or not, nobody notices or cares.

Compare that feeling to when you've achieved, and a leader or fellow colleague notices and takes the time to say, "Thank you so much for your hard work on that, I really appreciate it," or, "Well done, I can see you put everything into that project." You feel positive and valued, don't you? Your self-confidence increases and you begin to enjoy your overall job just that little bit more. Isn't it also true that immediately following this demonstration of appreciation, the quality of your work would be likely to increase? You might take just a little bit more care and put a little bit more effort into trying to recreate that reaction again.

This is the power of appreciation. I've heard many leaders say, "Yes, but that is their job, that's what they are paid to do." And yes, that is correct. However, regardless of what the facts are, there are still people involved, which means there are emotions involved. My response to that is to ask the question, "How much does it cost you to demonstrate your appreciation?"

Think of it like acknowledging the behaviour of a child. If you continually reprimand a child for poor behaviour and never acknowledge when they behave as you'd like, they will learn that to get attention, they must behave poorly. If you acknowledge them when they behave well, they will learn that to get the attention they desire they must repeat that positive behaviour.

Appreciation is simply demonstrating gratitude or recognising a desired action or result.

This can be as simple as saying "Thank you." These words go a long way in making someone feel good. As mentioned above, it's the same as children; the behaviour you focus on the most, that gives them the most attention, will be the behaviour you will see more of. So ensure that you are rewarding the good behaviour more than the poor behaviour.

'Thank you' can be expressed in person, on a hand written note or even in an email. It will leave your team member feeling more empowered, positive and enthusiastic to do it again next time and will therefore be more productive.

If you wanted to demonstrate your appreciation in an even more powerful way, then recognise the individual's characteristic that they used to produce this result at the same time. For example: "Thank you so much for completing that project, it really shows your commitment to the team's success." The completion of the project is the 'action' you are appreciating, and the 'commitment' is the individuals characteristic you are appreciating.

By doing this, you will give them the power to access this commitment more readily in the future. Thus, they will be even more committed to the team. This makes it easy to get your team to behave in the way you want them to, through catching them doing something right and showing your appreciation. Even though appreciation seems like such a small concept, whether you do it or not will have a great impact on your bottom line.

ACTIVITY:

If you don't naturally demonstrate your appreciation, then make it a habit to diarise it on a daily or weekly basis to search for something to appreciate and communicate it. A great side effect of doing this is that you will feel great when you've done it also.

Emotional Credit or Debt

Have you, or someone you know, ever been in an environment where you feel like you constantly *give* and the leader/business constantly *takes* with nothing in return? It can be an extremely demoralising, energy sucking and frustrating environment to work in. The culture and environment declines rapidly, until the team has nothing left to give. They will then do the bare minimum, so productivity is at its lowest and the cost of sick days takes a toll on the business, as they seem to miraculously increase.

The overall success of your business is comprised of the performance of each individual in your business. An individual can only be successful when they are feeling safe, emotionally supported and balanced.

I've seen it many times, and actually experienced it myself before I became a leader. The leader complains that the team is unproductive and is therefore frustrated. Out of this frustration, the leader leaves, blaming everyone else for the poor results. As a result, the remaining team steps up and becomes productive resulting in greater success than they were previously experiencing.

I whole-heartedly believe that the sole reason this happens is because the team members have a depleted 'emotional bank account'. The leader spent their entire time, telling them off for everything they do wrong, telling them they need to improve their performance, but giving them no strategies to improve with. They are constantly questioned about every move and rarely, if at all, are they ever caught doing something right, let alone congratulated or recognised for doing something well.

So, how does 'Emotional Credit and Debt' work? Well, how does a bank account work? You make deposits and you make withdrawals. What would you classify as a healthy bank account? It would be one that is in credit, which has money in it and the more money the healthier it would be. What would you class as an unhealthy bank account? It would be one that has no money in it, or even worse, has gone into deficit. If you keep making withdrawals, does money magically appear, to fill it up automatically, or do you need to work to make the deposits to fill it up again? (Well, if you won the lottery maybe, but typically, you need to work at it, right?)

As a bank account operates, so do the emotions of your people. When you first meet a new team member, you are opening a new emotional bank account. In order to get it started, you must make a deposit.

An example of a deposit is when you:

- Appreciate them.
- Recognise and compliment them on a job well done.
- Thank them for their hard work.
- Have a laugh with them.
- Help them identify their error and rectify it.
- Ask why they chose the behaviour (if you need to reprimand) before telling them off.
- Offer to help them cover their shift so they can go to a special event.
- Say thank you to them for volunteering to cover someone else's shift.
- A thank you note/flower etc.

- Say 'no' and then explaining the reasons and check for understanding.
- Acknowledge when they do something great.
- Thank them for going above and beyond.
- Show appreciation when they deserve it.
- Validate them when they are concerned or stressed.
- Listen in order to understand what they are saying and respond to them (not what you think they said or what the stock-standard line is).
- Have eye contact, and give them your full attention.
- Show them that you want to help them be successful ALWAYS.
- Reprimand in private, and praise in public, never embarrass or belittle someone in front of anyone else. (Never do it full stop but especially not in public.)
- Say 'yes' when you can, never say 'no' just for the use of your 'power'.
- Essentially catch your people doing the right thing, not the wrong thing and make it public.

Only when you have made enough deposits is it then okay to make a withdrawal and even then, the fewer withdrawals you make, the healthier their emotional bank account will be.

An example of a withdrawal is:

- Anything negative.
- Holding them accountable in a confronting way.
- Telling them off for something they have done, with no help for a solution.
- Being sarcastic or nasty to them (which is never ok).
- Giving them an off look or getting frustrated with them because they aren't as fast at something as you would be.

- Using a nasty tone.
- Asking them to cover someone else's shift without saying please or thank you.
- Not helping them if they request a day off.
- Not listening to them when they have a concern (no matter how trivial it may seem).
- Yelling at them.
- Saying 'no' with no valid reason – just because you have the title.
- Reprimanding them for being late without asking them what happened.
- Speaking to them when they are sick and asking them when they are coming back in, not how they are feeling and showing genuine concern for them.
- Ultimately, disrespecting them in any way.
- Reprimanding them for something you do/have done.

The best way to gauge where your team is at right now is to observe their attitude and behaviour, as this will be your barometer, indicating if their account is full or depleted. Ask yourself, "Are they in positive balance or negative balance, based on their behaviour and attitude?" Like a normal bank account, it won't automatically or instantly fix itself, to be in the positive, you must work to achieve that.

ACTIVITY:

Assess each of your team members' barometers and establish the health of their emotional bank account. Then highlight any depleted accounts and get to work! Again, if you need to diarise to do this, then do so. It will pay off in dividends – I promise.

Chapter 6:
Powerful
Conversations

"Seek first to understand, then to be understood."

~ Stephen Covey

As leaders, we may have heard the term "powerful conversations" used in a variety of contexts. Powerful conversations, from the DLT perspective, is all about making the conversation a *powerful* experience for the other person, where they receive your communication in a way that they can understand what you're saying, apply what you're guiding them to learn, and achieve the results they want to achieve.

Having a powerful conversation means that the person on the receiving end of your communication will walk away empowered and positive with a clear step-by-step plan, for what must be actioned.

In order to achieve this as a leader, you must:

- Listen to what's being said, rather than just hearing the words.
- Validate your team member where they are at, rather than just trying to move them forward.
- Develop your coaching skills by learning to ask great questions.

- Know how to have the tough conversations and when to have them.

This is the true art of communication, and learning and applying these principles is an essential step in the DLT model, because then you'll be ready to move on to developing your discipline style.

The Power of Listening

As a leader, you are juggling, talking to and taking action on requirements for your team, your customers, your suppliers, and the business itself, all whilst managing your own performance as well. You are constantly trying to keep all the balls in the air. It is very common for a leader to be doing 5 or 6 things – maybe even more – at the same time and it could be very easy to skim as much as you can to ensure you get it all done. Have you ever experienced this?

A common shortcut leaders often take is to continue working whilst having a conversation with a team member, or the commonly known 'walk and talk', when a team member approaches them to ask a question or discuss something. As leaders, what we forget to consider is how important the thing they need help with or want to discuss is to the individual.

Think about it from the other perspective for a moment. Have you ever had a conversation with someone and you knew they just weren't listening? They were either looking around, continued working, or you could see they were preoccupied with something else. Then when they respond, it's not even relevant to what you are saying. How does this make you feel? What is your perception of this person? What level of trust would you have for them? It's invalidating, isn't it. This person appears to be too busy, unable to help, not interested enough in anyone else's challenges to take a moment out to help. As this continues, your level of trust for this person diminishes, and you probably won't continue to communicate with them in the future if this happens often enough.

If we fast-forward 3 or 6 months and this occurrence is on repeat, it could lead the individual into a state of apathy. That is a precarious situation, as the team member feels that because the leader has no care for them, why should they care for their work, the customers or the team?

Another common habit leaders adopt is to formulate their response before the team member has finished speaking. This has the same outcome as not listening at all, because they either cut them short before they've finished speaking, or reply with an inappropriate answer.

An important aspect of leading an individual is the skill of listening. And yes, it is a skill, for reasons mentioned above. It's a highly under-rated skill which needs to be developed to ensure the leader continues to build and nurture the relationships they have with their people. When a person is really listened to and heard, they get bigger, they feel valued and their self-confidence grows. They emanate presence and feel safer, which leads to greater sense of trust.

One of the most profound experiences a human being can have is to be truly listened to. When the individual is completely present to you and curious about the next word you speak, their eyes are locked on you and body language is completely open. It's a rare but beautiful experience.

As Stephen Covey said so well, "*Seek first to understand, then to be understood.*" Place your priority on understanding your people, really listening to them. You can gain important insight into what's actually happening by listening to what they have to say, rather than coming up with your response before they've finished speaking. Listening is more than simply just nodding or agreeing, it's removing your own judgement and thought process to really hear what the other person is saying. It is also removing your own assumptions and interpretations about what is being said and becoming curious.

I get that this may seem quite unfamiliar in the beginning and it will absolutely take practise. To begin with, ask your team member to rate the importance of what they need to discuss with you on a scale of 1 to 10, 1 being not overly important and 10 being extremely important. This will help you prioritise whether you stop and let them continue, or ask if they can give you a moment while you finish what you are doing. Anything rated higher than a 7 would warrant stopping what you're doing as it's quite important to them. You will begin to learn each individuals rating scale and what's important as you apply this technique.

An easy way to begin practising your listening skills is to simply repeat back to them what you've heard them say, to clarify your understanding. Saying something like, "Okay, great, so what I've heard you say is … Is that right?" or, "What I'm sensing is that …" or, "Okay, so let me repeat back what I've heard you say."

This will do two things. Firstly, it will demonstrate to them that you were really listening to them, and secondly, help you clarify what is being said. When we take the time to do this at the beginning, it can save us ample time down the track from misunderstandings and mistakes due to miscommunication.

As you progress, work on taking off the 'I know' hat. The 'I know what you're about to say, I've heard it before and here's my stock-standard response' mindset. As discussed above, the 'I know' hat does nothing but break down the relationship between you and your team. Instead, be curious about what this individual is saying and how they came to this conclusion.

Maintain great eye contact with them, do not look over their shoulder or up in the air, be present to them. Stay still, don't fidget and move around unnecessarily. Be curious, again, put yourself in their shoes and ask questions about their situation.

Respond with, "Okay, tell me more," or, "What else?" or, "That sounds important to you, tell me more," to gather more information. Nod to encourage more conversation.

Allow silence immediately after they finish speaking. Often the gold in the communication is revealed after a pause, if you wait long enough to allow them to continue speaking should they think of something more to add. If they don't continue, ask them, "Is there anything else you'd like to add?"

Don't think about what you're going to have for dinner tonight or what someone else has just said to you, focus on the person you are conversing with. If you can't, then ask the person to wait for a moment while you address what's concerning you or make a note and gather your thoughts. Don't interrupt them, allow them to finish and then allow the silence.

It's not about getting it perfect first time. Remember the baby story, give yourself the grace to begin to apply this, one step at a time. By the time you have implemented each of these suggestions, you will truly be a Master Listener.

Successful Validation

In business, we work at great pace, always looking for the next sale, the next success, the next win. With the rapid pace of life, we are continually moving faster. This also applies to our communication. Everything we talk about, do and think about is usually about moving forward. As a leader we must learn to slow the pace down for ourselves and our people, so we can breathe, be present in the moment and, more importantly, learn from the current situation.

When we are forced to continue to jump from job to job, project to project, leave behind the mistakes and just look forward, we often miss the value in having had the experience. It's like we are on the never-ending spinning wheel of life and it doesn't slow down, it's only getting faster. When we feel unhappy or are struggling, it can be an indication that we need to stop, slow down and take a moment to breathe, reflect on where we're at, how we're feeling and how far we've come before we move on.

If a person is complaining, unhappy or is simply struggling with performance, our initial reaction can be to move them on, hurry them up, get them to focus on what they can do to improve. Whilst this is correct, there is a step prior to this that most leaders miss, which is validation.

As a leader, it's important to understand this, not only for our team, but also for ourselves, because the natural tendency for a leader is to work at lightning speed and focus on what's next, and next, and next. Working ourselves to the bone is not sustainable and doesn't benefit anyone, not ourselves, our team or our family, let alone the business. Because we are the leader, it's up to us to recognise this.

More often than not, when people are complaining or whinging about something, as leaders, we feel like we have to fix it, help them move past it or tell them to get over it and move on, which is all forward-moving conversation. You may, however, find that sometimes, they aren't asking you to fix it, they are not looking for a solution, they simply want to be heard and feel understood and validated.

A common mistake that many leaders make is to assume that they need to provide a solution and therefore jump to make excuses, find reasons or just brush over this concern without careful consideration of the issue.

Based on the Oxford Dictionary definition, validation is, "to recognise or affirm the validity or worth of (a person or their feelings or opinions)." In other words, to simply meet them where they are at, don't attempt to move them forward to a solution. When you validate, you're not moving them anywhere, you're simply staying present with them in that moment.

When someone appears to be complaining or whinging about something and you feel like they are using you to unload, you do not have to take it on or agree with it, but it is important to make them feel heard. You can do this without agreement by responding with something like, "Okay, tell me more." Once they have finished speaking, you can reply with a statement along the lines of, "Okay, I can see how you would feel that way."

Once you have heard what is being said, allow them the space in silence to reflect, process the validation and accept it. It may feel a little uncomfortable for you, but when they are in their own mind, they won't notice any length of silence.

In this time of silence, remove any need to defend yourself, the business or anything else, for that matter. Remember the importance of what your intention is for this conversation and what you'd like them to walk away thinking, knowing and feeling. This is not the time to defend; this is the time to validate. As I said, you don't need to agree with what they're saying, or even like it for that matter, but you must allow them to express their emotions without defence.

Once you can see that they have processed your validation, and start to look up, then you can ask them what they would like the outcome of this conversation to be. Simply ask them, "For what purpose are you telling me this?" and, "What would you like to walk away with from this conversation?" Once they have answered these questions, then you can determine your response from there. Often, they won't want anything to be done, they just want to be heard.

If you feel it's the right time, you can also ask them, "What actions are you willing to take to resolve this?" You'll know it's the right time if their demeanour has lifted and they have replied with a clear answer about what they'd like the outcome to be.

6 Steps to Successful Validation:

1. Listen to them speak, be curious by saying, "Tell me more."
2. Repeat back what you've heard once they've finished.
3. Reply with, "Okay, I can see how/why you are feeling that."
4. Silence, for as long as they need.
5. Remove any feelings for the need to defend (they will not serve you).
6. Once they have processed the validation, you can use moving forward language like:
   - "What would you like the outcome of this to be?"
   - Ask what actions they are willing to take to resolve this issue.

Developing Your Coaching Skills

When you are leading people while running a business, while trying to achieve your own goals, your most limited resource is time. Most leaders experience this and try to be everything to everyone all of the time. This means that when a team member asks a question or is looking for a new strategy, the leader can fall into the trap of giving the answer straight away. The trap is well disguised, as they think that this is saving everyone time, however it's actually extending the length of time it will take the team member to learn, costing even more time.

I remember an experience I had as a leader. I'd had a breakthrough solving a problem that I had for the prior 6 months. I was so excited that I rang my area manager looking for a congratulations or a well done, and to my surprise, the response was "I've only been telling you that for the last 6 months." Whilst this was the case and she had said it to me over and over, I didn't hear what she was saying, I didn't understand and therefore had no ownership of the idea. My unconscious mind dismissed it and it didn't become a part of my awareness. It was only when I came up with the idea myself that I thought it was the best idea in the world, and was willing and able to take action. Have you ever had a similar experience?

When we establish our own ideas, we have the greatest amount of ownership of them, which gives us the greatest chance of implementing them and achieving the desired outcome. As a leader, the skillset required to enable this is coaching. Coaching in leadership is predominantly asking questions with a splash of suggestions based on your experience and expertise.

One of the most malleable coaching models is the I.G.R.O.W. model. Whilst it is a basic coaching model which helps you with questioning skills so you know where you're at in the conversation, don't be misled by its simplicity, it's extremely powerful in a range of different scenarios. It can be used in a typical 'one-on-one' performance-developing conversation, or a brief 'on the go' conversation. It can also be used when dealing with customer complaints, to resolve issues between team members, or even as a model to base your meeting agenda on. Essentially, you can apply it in any conversational situation.

So let's take a look at the model:

I **is for Intention.** As we've already discussed in this book, setting your intention for any communication, especially coaching, will give you the greatest opportunity of achieving the desired outcome. In the I.G.R.O.W model, setting your intention can be either with yourself or the individual or team you are communicating with, establishing what you'd like to achieve as a result of this communication. It may be to establish a clear action plan or to help the team come to a resolution, or to help this individual find a new way of behaving to achieve different results.

G is for Goal. This part of the model is focused on helping the individual work out what their desired goal or outcome is. A goal is something which is specific and measurable. Whereas the Intention is what will happen during this communication, the Goal is what will be achieved, as a result of the conversation but not necessarily by the end of the conversation, as there may be a series of steps and actions to take over time, to achieve the goal. If we're not clear on what we want to achieve, then we have minimal chance of achieving it. It's important to note here that it's not a step-by-step process. You don't have to ask the first question, then the second and so on. It must be a natural flowing conversation. These questions are simply suggestions to get you started, to build a 360 degree all senses fired picture of what it looks like for this person, once they have achieved their outcome.

Examples:

"What is your desired outcome?"

"What would you like to achieve?"

"For what purpose would you like to achieve this?"

"What will achieving this give you?"

"What will you miss out on if you don't achieve this?"

"What is the purpose of us having this conversation?"

"What would you like to walk away knowing, thinking and feeling after this conversation?"

"When you've achieved it, what does it look like?"

"How does it feel, once you've achieved it?"

"What will others say to you?"

"What will you be telling yourself?"

The more questions you can ask to give the individual clarity on what their desired outcome is, the better. It may feel like you are repeating yourself, which is okay. Remember that given a big enough reason why, the how will look after itself. The goal is their 'why'. It's the big picture that's going to pull them through all the tasks they must complete to achieve it. The clearer they are in the goal section, the easier the rest of the conversation will be.

R **is for Reality.** This part of the model is to establish where they currently are in relation to their goal. Again, the conversation must flow, it's not a step-by-step questionnaire. So go with what feels natural.

Examples:

"Okay, so what is the situation right now?

"What are the facts we currently know?"

"What are the numbers right now?"

"How do you know this to be true?"

"What is the evidence stating that this is the situation right now?"

"So, where are you right now in relation to this goal?"

"What are you currently experiencing?"

"What does it feel like right now?"

"What does it look like?"

"What are people currently saying to you?"

"What are you telling yourself about this situation right now?"

O is for Options. This is the fun part of the model because you can go crazy, exploring and searching for all the different opportunities and possibilities they have to achieve this outcome. The crazier you get, the more likely they are to achieve it. There is no stupid idea, everything is worth writing down. Again, you don't have to ask every suggested question, simply keep it natural and milk out as many ideas as you can.

Examples:

"Okay, if there was nothing stopping you, what could you do to achieve this?"

"What is just one thing you could do to move towards your goal?"

"If you were in a land of pure potential where everything was possible, what could you do?"

"If you were Wonder Woman/Superman, what could you do?"

"If everything was stacked in your favour, what would be possible?"

"If you had all the answers, what would be your first step?"

"If you knew exactly what to do, where would you start?"

"If you had a magic wand, what would you create?"

Whilst these seem like pretty 'wacky' questions, the purpose of them is to get the brain thinking outside the box. When the brain switches from logical to creative, we can problem solve much more efficiently.

They will most likely push back in this section and say, "I don't know." This is great, because it means they've reached the boundary of their current thinking. When they push through, you will be helping them establish new streams of thinking and new solutions.

The way you do this is to simply ask, "What else?" over and over again. Do not accept an "I don't know." Commit and push them to come up with another idea. Ask them to repeat what they say, to cement the new thinking. Once they believe they are finished, get them to come up with another 3 to 5 options by asking them, "What else?" You can even say something like, "Let's get crazy, let's really think outside the box. If anything were possible, what could you do? What could be another option?" Keep going until you're satisfied that there's a workable plan in there to help them achieve their goal.

W is for Way Forward. Now you are moving to the pointy end of the conversation, this is where you review the list of all the options you have created and establish a plan of action to move forward with.

Examples:

"Okay, so looking at all of the options you have come up with, what is possible?"

"Of all the ideas here, which one would you like to implement?"

"If you were to select just one idea to progress you towards your goal, which one would it be?"

"What else" – you can ask this question as many times as you like to help them get clear on what their specific action plan is. Don't stop until you are absolutely clear on what the plan is, because if you're not clear then chances are they won't be clear either.

These are just a few ideas to help them pinpoint what their specific action plan will be and what steps they need to take to achieve the goal. Make sure, in this part of the process, they are documenting the ideas and action plan. It's important that they write, not you, because they will own their notes and the plan and will be more likely to implement the actions.

There is a massive caveat on this. There is, however, a really important factor here that, if you don't consider it, could work against you. You must consider the team member's level of experience. You couldn't sit a brand new team member down and say, "So what are your key KPI's?" They wouldn't have a clue what you're talking about. So if they are 'incompetent' when it comes to what you're asking, that's when you need to take the time to sit down and explain it to them.

TEACHING SOMETHING NEW:

Because your time is extremely valuable, you must set the standard that, unless they have a pen and their notepad in hand, they are wasting your time. (Obviously there's a way to say it that doesn't make them feel bad.) But DO NOT start teaching them something until they have this in hand, ready to scribe. Here is a simple formula to teach effectively:

- Explain once.
- Explain and demonstrate by doing it yourself (they take notes).
- Ask them to explain to you.
- Ask them to demonstrate to you by following their notes.

This may feel like it takes a long time, however taking the time to do this well the first time round will save you so much time and possibly even money down the track.

Asking Coaching Questions In A Meeting:

Have you ever experienced a meeting where the leader begins with lots of information sharing, then they launch into the plan for the day, and tell everyone what the goals are and what needs to happen. When the leader stops talking, all you can hear is crickets (silence). Everyone is still waking up, needing a coffee, or worried about a problem they have to deal with. The leader has the right intention, and it's very clear and easy to understand for them, but everyone else in the team has no idea what's just been said.

How do you change this, I hear you ask? You must ask questions. You must give the ownership back to your team members. The amount to which they have ownership will be the extent of their implementation and success.

Rather than telling everyone what to do, set the clear expectation of what you want them to bring to the meeting about their role.

For example:

Information About Their Two Most Important KPI's.

Current KPI 1:

_____

Current KPI 2:

_____

Goal KPI 1:

_____

Goal KPI 2:

_____

Most urgent action to achieve goal KPI 1:

_____

Most urgent action to achieve goal KPI 2:

_____

They must give a snapshot analysis of their role from the past week and identify what action they will take to achieve their KPI goals this week.

Then as a team, you can ask them to articulate how they are going to improve that KPI this week. With that, you expect them to come up with the answers. They may even come up with answers they hadn't thought about yet. When you get the conversation flowing, you may also find that other people share their own successes or wins, which may help them. You could also initiate this by getting those strong in one area to help the others weak in that area to come up with some ideas.

When they are coming up with the ideas to action for improvement, you will see far better results than if you were to sit there and tell them what to do.

How To Have Tough Conversations

Everything we have discussed up until now is about who you need to be, implementing effective communications skills, and setting clear expectations to ensure you give yourself the best opportunity for success as a leader. However, if you fail to maintain expectations and hold your people accountable, then no matter who you're being and what you do, it won't work long-term. Setting clear expectations and holding people to account is essential for your success.

For example: imagine there was a customer with a complaint and your team member was having a bad day. They couldn't be bothered helping them, so they just did the bare minimum to get the customer off the phone. They found that worked because there was no consequence to their actions. The next time the team member can't be bothered, they remember what worked last time. This time, they are even more short with the customer on the phone because they know that works.

The third time the team member is asked a difficult question that they don't know the answer to, the easy option could be to just hang up, so they do. This would be appalling customer service, to say the least, but if you get the wrong customer, at minimum it may end up as a costly customer complaint, and at worse, you may end up in court or you could have a current affairs show on your doorstep. Either way, it's not going to be a situation you enjoy dealing with.

It is for that reason that when something is not done as per your minimum expectations, it must be addressed immediately. If it's not addressed, like in the example, the behaviour just gets worse and worse and you end up with unhappy customers, unhappy staff and your business gains a bad reputation. If that goes unaddressed, it could lead to the failure of the business. I know this is an extreme example, but I chose it for a reason, because too often we let the small things slide, thinking, "Oh well, it doesn't matter this time." A reason we leave it could be because we want to avoid confrontation. As you can see in this example, having the initial conversation with your team member will be less confrontational than the conversation you need to have with an irate customer.

As I've mentioned before, most people will take the shortest route possible to the end, regardless of whether it gets them to their desired outcome or not. This is because it is human nature to do more to avoid pain than to gain pleasure. If there are no consequences to taking the short cut, then they'll most likely do this every time. So if you want your people to be successful, you must make it more painful for them to not perform or not do what is expected than it is to do their job well the first time and meet or exceed expectations.

This means addressing them when they do not meet expectations or do their job as required. What's important here is that you remain consistent and take action every single time an offence occurs. This is not about being a nag or making life difficult for your team, it's about helping them achieve their greatest potential. This is why it's important to be clear on your intention before you begin a tough conversation. If you simply want to tell them off, then you won't achieve your desired outcome. If your intention is to hold them accountable and give them the best chance of success then your communication will more than likely be well-received.

A tough conversation is simply acknowledging the behaviour. It is a conversation where you highlight the person's behaviour and then reference the expectations section that relates to this behaviour. It certainly is not heated and doesn't involve anger and yelling. In fact, the more you can keep emotion out of this conversation, the more successful you will be at getting the desired outcome. There are varying degrees of tough conversations, where you start with the coaching approach and build (if the behaviour continues) until it turns into performance management.

FIRST TIME: "The Coaching Conversation."

1. Determine your desired outcome and set the intention for the conversation. This takes a little practice, but most of the time it will simply be to make the team member aware of their behaviour and how it is not in line with your minimum expectations. For example: I want to help them see that dismissing customers' concerns by doing the bare minimum will not help her/him get to the goals they/we have.

2. See yourself as a detective. You must find out all the facts before you form an opinion about what and how it should have been handled. You do this by asking something like, "Tell me about..." (whatever the behaviour was). For example: "Tell me about your interaction with that customer." Remember that

excuses are not acceptable. Whatever happened, the customer must take first precedence. After all, that's how you get paid. No customers = no jobs for anyone.

3. Once they have explained the circumstances, ask yourself, "Is that in line with your expectations? How would you have handled that situation?" Always remember there are 2 sides to every story. Your goal here is to hold them to your standard. Reference the applicable minimum expectation and ask them, "Is there anything you don't understand about the expectations? Do you need anything clarified?"

4. Reference your vision, their individual goal and the expectations you've set to achieve that, and ask, "Is that in line with what we are trying to achieve here?" For example: "Is that behaviour going to help you achieve your/our goal of ...?"

5. Ask them if they can think of another way they could have handled it. For example: "Can you think of another way you could have handled the situation that would have led to a different/more positive outcome?"

6. Then ask, "What about another way?" Get them to come up with 2 or 3 different ways they could have handled it to get a more positive outcome. You're helping them build a new way of thinking, so they have options to choose from next time something like this happens. You are also letting them know that by making this situation a coaching conversation, it will be shorter and easier for them to just do their job properly next time, rather than having to have this full conversation afterwards.

7. Review your minimum expectations. Is this situation covered in them? Do you need to add it?

SECOND TIME: (Same scenario)

If the behaviour is repeated and there has been no improvement following the prior conversation then you begin to get a bit tougher with some more stern language.

1. Set Intention as before. This time add, "To make it clear that this behaviour is unacceptable," and ask again: "Is there anything you don't understand about the expectations? Do you need anything clarified?"

2. Be the detective. Find out what happened from the team member's perspective (again, not accepting excuses).

3. Reference your last conversation about this. "How did you apply what you learned last time?"

4. Regardless of their response (as you know they didn't apply anything), explain to them clearly and sternly, "That behaviour is not acceptable in this team. Is there anything you don't understand about our minimum expectations? Is there anything preventing you from meeting the minimum expectations?"

5. Advise that if it should happen again, you will be forced to begin performance management.

THIRD TIME: "Private Official Meeting"

1. Get clear on your desired outcome from the meeting you are about to have.

2. Remove yourselves from the work environment for a private meeting.

3. State the situation as you/customer sees it. Ask, "Is there any incorrect information here?"

4. Document any differing information so they know this is serious and you will be clarifying with the customer.

5. Ask, "For what purpose did you choose your displayed behaviour?"

6. Ask, "How do you feel/think now about your behaviour?"

7. Regardless of whether they are remorseful or not, you must document their responses to the following:

    • "What actions are you going to take to ensure this will not happen again?"

    • "What help do you need (from you or others) to ensure that it doesn't happen again?"

    • "Is there anything else preventing you from making these changes?"

    • Write down the agreed action steps and you both sign it as an agreed action plan.

8. Thank them and release them from the meeting. You remain there to review your notes and add anything else you need to ensure they are thorough and accurate.

9. Give them a copy of the action plan that is signed.

FOURTH TIME:

Repeat third time and add at the end:

"Should this happen again, your position in this team will be questioned and official performance management will begin."

Ensure that your notes are documented clearly with a specific action plan.

Tip:

To ensure that I didn't allow my emotions to get in the way, I always imagined that their mother/father/partner was standing right beside them when I had these conversations. That helped me remain accountable to them and ensured that

I was being firm but fair at all times. Remember that you will get the best out of this person when they are feeling happy and empowered, so the goal is always to help them return to that state.

In General

Ask yourself the question, "Is it behaviour or attitude that is causing the problem?"

Behaviour:

If it's a problem with their behaviour, then your conversation could go something like this:

"I have become aware of this particular behaviour." (Explain.) "This is not in line with minimum standards/expectations. Please explain to me the reason for your choice of behaviour."

"What is your solution?"

"Moving forward, what will you choose to do differently?"

Attitude:

If it's a problem with their attitude then bring it back to purpose. Ask, "Why are you here?"

Never lead with fear of losing them, because you are holding them to expectation. If they leave, know you are better to have a team of brand new people in your business who love what they do and want to be there, rather than a team of experienced people who have a 'can't be bothered' attitude. Know your expectations around attitude and presence, and communicate them. If they fall below those expectations, then acknowledge it with them immediately! Never accept anything less! The key to all of this is that you must ALWAYS display the attitude you expect of your team.

Your Approach:

If it is a severe offence against the expectations, then give advance warning that there will be a conversation about the issue. This gives them time to think about their behaviour and you the time to prepare the conversation and how it will go in your mind, as well as get clear on what the consequence will be.

If it's a minor offence then jump on it immediately. The most effective feedback is at the time of behaviour. Ensure you are clear on what the evidence of the consultant not performing is. Be very clear. This will be straight-forward after having set very clear expectations. It can't be reiterated enough: know your desired outcome, what do you want them to walk away knowing, thinking, feeling? Have a few ideas in mind to help them fix the problem. Be prepared with the consequence.

YOU MUST ALWAYS FOLLOW THROUGH WITH THE CONSEQUENCE

Managing Conflict

When any group of people operate in the same space for long periods of time, there are bound to be issues and conflicts that arise. Your ability to manage these differences will determine the quality of your environment. If you allow conflict to continue without addressing it, it can damage your environment. As you will see further on in this book, a positive work environment is essential for success.

But before I explain how to manage the differences, I need to remind you about chunk levels and that different people are comfortable with different sized 'units' of information. This can be what causes differing opinions and behaviours between people, so as a leader you need to understand how to manage that. If you need a reminder, go back to the section in chapter 2, *Understanding the Concept of Chunking.*

As we discussed, this is how we communicate all of the time. So when you understand that we all have a preferred 'chunk' level, then you can help people when they experience miscommunication or have a disagreement.

So let's say you have a team member (John) who is frustrated because he feels like he is doing all the work with customers, while another team member (Jack) doesn't appear to be doing any work to help the team, he's just doing his own work. It has come to a head and you need to get involved because they are at each other's throats and it's affecting the environment. You must first be in the right environment and set the tone of the conversation by setting some clear expectations.

- Make sure you're in an environment where you won't be interrupted by other team members or customers.
- One person speaks at a time.
- Explain that they may only speak with 'I feel' statements.

An 'I feel' statement prevents anyone from feeling attacked and no one is justified in responding in an attacking manner because there is no right or wrong with feelings. How someone feels is right for them.

Ask them one at a time.

Me: For what purpose are you concerned about this?

John: I feel frustrated because our customers aren't being served because Jack is doing his own work and not helping out.

Me: Okay, so for what purpose would you like our customers to be served?

John: So we give great customer service to all of our customers and so I can get my work done too.

Me: And why do we want to give great customer service to all of our customers and why would you want to get your work done too?

John: So I can provide good customer service and we are successful and achieve our vision or goal.

As you can see, you're chunking him up to a higher level.

Then you ask Jack the same questions:

Me: For what purpose are you spending a lot of time doing your own work?

Jack: So I make sure my work is accurate.

Me: Okay, and for what purpose do you want your work to be accurate?

Jack: So that I have happy customers.

Me: And for what purpose would you want to have happy customers?

Jack: So that I contribute to the team achieving our vision or goal.

Now obviously, it's not going to pan out exactly like this, and they most likely won't use exactly the same words, so you must listen carefully for the similarities in their language. They will be there.

Can you see what just happened? If you chunk them up high enough to the bigger, more abstract level of information, they will both get to the same point eventually. It's just that they have taken a different view point to get there.

Me: Oh, ok, so did you just hear that? You both want the same thing. Well, that's great you both care so much. Now we need to look at what specifically we can do to help both parties.

You then chunk them back down only as far as you can with agreement.

Me: Okay, so how specifically can we fix John's concern?

You could ask John and Jack separately and find out what they think. Then ask the opinion of the other team member to see if they think that would work or where the pitfalls are. You continue this process until they come to the agreement for a plan to move forward. You could also look at the facts and assess whether there is validity in John's concerns. Maybe a solution needs to be some time management for Jack. Another solution might be looking at what the rest of the team are doing if John is the only one working with customers.

The key here is that you see yourself as the 'facilitator'. You don't have to come up with the answers, you don't need to know it all in this situation. All you are doing is asking them questions so they can see that they really are both on the same page and then asking them what they think the solution could be.

The Model of Questioning:

1. Ask the first person any range of the following questions:

a. For what purpose...?

b. So why do you want that?

c. What will this give you?

Repeat as many times as necessary to get them to a broad enough abstract point of view. You'll know when you get there.

2. Ask the second person any range of the following questions:

a. For what purpose...?

b. So why do you want that?

c. What will this give you?

Repeat as many times as you need to get them to a broad enough abstract point of view that is similar to the first person. You'll know when you get there.

3. Recognise and state when they get to the same broad abstract point of view.

4. Now you need to chunk them back down to the smallest point with both parties' agreement. Ask them questions like the below in any order, as many times as you need to:

a. How specifically can we fix this?
b. What specifically can be done here?
c. What is a possible solution to the problem?

Hand them back the problem, and expect them to come up with the solution. Know this: for the problem to exist, so must the solution. Have certainty that they CAN absolutely find the solution. Do not settle for, "I don't know." That's not an acceptable response. The benefit of doing this is a) They are the ones doing the hard work to find the solution, and b) You're teaching them to come up with their own solutions, which means they won't get in the habit of dumping their problems on you.

> To download your very own complimentary copy of the I.G.R.O.W. coaching template to use in your coaching sessions, go to www.leadershipskillsreducethebills.com

PART 3
Discipline

Chapter 7:
Managing You

"If a man can control his own mind, he can find his own way to enlightenment, and all wisdom and virtue will naturally come to him."

~ Buddha

Sometimes discipline can seem like such a difficult or boring concept. After all, who has fun when they're disciplined? Well, let me share with you, when you are on purpose and you are succeeding and achieving the goals you desire, you absolutely will be having fun. Before you get to have the results though, you must demonstrate a level of discipline to do what must be done to achieve those goals.

The easiest way to be disciplined is to remain connected to your 'why' – your purpose as a leader – and understand how and what drives you to get the results you desire.

In this chapter, we'll explore:

- Gaining clarity on your purpose in leadership
- The roller coaster ride of motivation
- Merely surviving or thriving

This chapter is all about the 'being' of discipline, which we now know must come first. Once we've completed the 'being' section, we'll be able to move into the 'doing' section of discipline.

Time To Gain Clarity On Your Purpose in Leadership

At the beginning of this book, we talked about being clear on your why, your purpose in life, what gets you out of bed in the morning. Well now we're going to chunk it down, to specifically explore your purpose as a leader. Let's take a look at why you became a leader and what being a leader in your environment gives you.

'Given a big enough reason why, the how will look after itself.'

When you understand your 'why' – otherwise known as 'your purpose as a leader' – the mundane tasks you have to do, all become worthwhile, as you know that it's all leading you to a greater picture. There's no greater reason to be clear on your purpose as a leader than to motivate you towards your vision, the picture of your success. Remember the concept of chunking? Well, in order to run a successful business, you must be disciplined. Knowing your purpose will help you remain disciplined.

Imagine a working environment where people just rock up when they want, have a chat, then once the work day starts they head over to the coffee machine and get a coffee. Half an hour later they make it to their desk and turn on the computer, only to find there is an urgent email that required attention first thing in the morning. At this time the phone rings and they haven't got time to answer it, so it rings out. Customers are calling, wanting what was promised to them, and everyone is just plain grumpy!

As the leader, you receive a text message an hour after the official start time from a team member who is not coming in today because they are sick. This puts more pressure on the team and makes them even grumpier.

Can you imagine that day? As the leader, how would you be feeling? How do you think the team would be feeling and, arguably more important, how would your customers be feeling? Everyone would be pretty unhappy, wouldn't they? This is a result of an undisciplined environment.

- No clear start time and no consequences if they arrive late.
- No meeting to set up the intention for the day.
- No communication to see who's got what on for the day.
- No preparation before you open for business.
- No expectation around social chit-chats whilst making coffee.
- No standard when it comes to calling in sick.
- This is not a team that will achieve any level of sustainable success.

So how do you remain focused on your discipline?

As the leader, you create your environment and your discipline has a big impact on the environment. Whilst we aren't at the environment section yet, this point is essential to helping you build an amazing environment for you and your people.

Imagine an environment where the leader doesn't want to be at work. If that's the case, then I can guarantee you, the team don't either. An environment like this will never lead to a successful and profitable team. The bad news is that the environment is your responsibility, so it's your job to fix it if it's not right. The good news is that you have the power to change it because you are the leader.

Because you are the leader, you are expected to be motivated and happy ALL of the time, regardless of what the current environment is like. What's going on behind the scenes or in your personal life is irrelevant. The best way to get you through any tough days on your way to creating an amazing environment is to focus on your 'purpose' or your 'why'.

I don't know of one leader who has achieved anything worth mentioning who's had an easy ride to success. There are always challenges, and it's not the challenges that cause you to succeed or fail. It's how you learn to deal with them. Here is a simple model of questions to answer to help you get clear on your purpose as a leader:

What do you enjoy most about being a leader?

_____

_____

_____

What makes you feel good about being a leader?

_____

_____

_____

Who, as a leader, inspires you? What characteristics do you admire most in them? You may know them personally or you may know of them.

_____

_____

_____

What aspect of your role as a leader are you passionate about?

_____

_____

_____

What are you good at? This is about singing your praises, blowing your own trumpet. Don't be embarrassed or shy, be proud of what you are good at. Make a list of at least 6 things that you are good at as a leader.

_____

_____

_____

What areas do people ask you for help in as a leader?

_____

_____

_____

What do others say you're good at?

_____

_____

_____

What makes you unique? This is in relation to your personality, your skillset, your previous experience – ANYTHING that makes you, you! Find as many things as you can that set you apart from others that you are proud of.

_____

_____

_____

What do you want to be remembered for as a leader long after you're gone?

_____

_____

_____

If you could teach a new leader one aspect of leadership, what would it be?

_____

_____

_____

What values are most important to you as a leader? Select a maximum of 5 from the list of suggestions, or add your own:

Achievement	Dedication	Goals
Adventure	Discipline	Game Plan
Accessibility	Determination	Growth
Authenticity	Diversity	Habits
Advancement	Democracy	Honesty
Autonomy	Directness	Happiness
Brave	Empowerment	Integrity
Being the Best	Education	Independence
Belief	Environment	Innovation
Clarity	Exclusivity	Inspiration
Certainty	Ethical	Involvement
Change	Equality	Influence
Communication	Enthusiasm	Joy
Contribution	Efficiency	Justice
Connection	Expertise	Kindness
Creativity	Excellence	Knowledge
Commitment	Fairness	Lead By Example
Comfort	Focus	Learning
Collaborative	Friendship	Loyalty
Customer Delight	Fun	Motivation
Confidence	Flexibility	Money
Decisiveness	Freedom	Merit

Nurture	Perfection	Timeliness
Natural Obedience	Responsibility	Teaching
Ownership	Risk Taking	Trustworthy
Optimistic	Reliability	Unique
Openness	Respect	Understanding
Order	Realistic	Unity
Patience	Resourceful	Vision
Philanthropy	Stability	Variety
Persistence	Significance	Value
Passionate	Security	Wisdom
Productivity	Service	Winning
Play	Status	Wealth
Performance	Truth	

_____

_____

_____

What challenges have you overcome or are you overcoming as a leader?

_____

_____

_____

If you were to send a message to a large group of people about leadership, what would it be?

_____

_____

_____

Well done on pushing through to get those answers. I understand that looking at yourself from that perspective can be difficult at times. However, it's getting yourself to do the things you don't want to do that makes you great. As you know it's in the difficulties that you learn and grow as a leader. Great job!!

Review the answers to these questions. Is there a theme? Is there a word that stands out across many of the questions? Has something struck you as you've explored these answers as to why you are committed to being a great leader? Look at the answers to the questions and look for what stands out. What words speak directly to your heart? What makes your heart sing from these answers? It may not come to you immediately, so leave it for a day or so and then see what jumps out at you. Based on your answers to these questions, you will be able to piece together your big reason *why*.

What's important is that your purpose in leadership must be something that is actionable, that is within your control to do on a daily basis, rather than an outcome determined by something outside of you.

So after reviewing your answers, come up with one sentence that drives you as a leader. You're aiming for this sentence to be the one that gives you butterflies in your tummy, that excites you! This is your purpose as a leader:

_____

_____

_____

Now, carry it with you every day. Write it on a coloured piece of paper, stick in on your screen, do whatever you need to do to ensure that you remember your driving force. So when you experience a challenge, have a tough decision to make or simply need inspiration, you can revisit this note and reconnect with your *purpose* as a leader!

The Roller Coaster Ride Of Motivation

As I've already explained earlier in this book, what you focus on and talk about will have a great impact on your results. It is the same when you explore how you are motivated.

Many people draw their motivation from what it is they don't want. The pain of being where they don't want to be is what inspires them to take rapid action. This can be a great tool to use, however unless you understand how you are motivated, you could fall into the trap of producing inconsistent results. Inconsistency is your enemy, because regardless of the positive action you take, if you have a reputation of being inconsistent then your people will lack a sense of trust for you and find it difficult to believe what you say. Trust is crucial to building a successful, sustainable team environment.

Have you ever got to a point where things are so painful that you make a decision to change? "That's it. I'm done, I'm no longer going to put up with this!" It often happens in the context of wanting to lose weight.

In the beginning, you are so fired up that you are inspired to jump out of bed to exercise and not eat any bad foods. When you're offered, you may respond with, "No, thank you," and you're thinking, "No, thank you, because I don't want to be fat." As this pattern continues, you start to see some results. Your jeans are getting a bit looser, you've got a bit more energy and you're feeling pretty good about yourself.

Over time, as you start to notice positive results, when you're offered that cake or a coffee date when you should be at the gym, your response starts to be, "Oh, yeah, okay, I've been pretty good lately." This repeated in turn sees you begin to create a new pattern of skipping some of your exercising and healthy eating habits because after all, you have been good.

As a result, you begin to slip back into the old routine. The jeans are getting tighter, clothes are hugging a bit more, and potentially you're feeling less energetic, until you've put on the weight you lost and you're back at square one. It is like a roller coaster: up, down, up, down.

This is because you are motivated by what you don't want, and when you get away from where you don't want to be, there is no more motivation to keep going, so you stop taking action, because you're no longer motivated, giving you inconsistent results. So whilst 'away' motivation may be what springs you into action, it's also important to be clear on what it is you do want so you can then make the flip to refocus and continue to progress towards that picture or goal.

This can happen in the workplace too. As an example, we may get to a point where we are sick of the negativity or the underperformance. We get so fired up, we make a decision to address all issues or situations that relate to creating a negative environment and underperformance.

In the beginning we take action, we address every issue, hold our people accountable and communicate our expectation around negativity and underperformance. Then, as time passes and you are enjoying the lack of negativity and underperformance, little issues that happen begin to go unnoticed. You justify in your mind, 'Oh, they've been so good, I won't pull them up on it, this time, or, They've got it, they know,' which sends an unconscious message to your people that they no longer have to be disciplined because you won't address it.

You've been motivated enough to get the team out of the negative and underperforming mentality but you haven't refocused on where you now want to take your team, what you are now motivated to move towards. It is in this moment that you must make the switch to work towards the environment you do want to create for your people.

This is why it is imperative to be *very* clear on what you are motivated towards, what your purpose is as a leader and what the business/team vision or picture of success is. When you are clear on what you are motivated towards, you can easily make the switch, stop producing inconsistent results and begin to enjoy moving towards the amazing environment you want to create.

Merely Surviving Or Thriving?

Do you know what it's like to feel safe? Do you live in a home you feel safe in? Do you have a family or a relationship where you feel safe? It is a reassuring feeling when you feel safe in your external environment. It gives you the ability to focus on other things that may empower you and are important to you, doesn't it? You are able to thrive.

Have you ever felt unsafe in a situation you were unfamiliar with? Have you ever felt uncertain in a relationship or with your finances? It's consuming, isn't it? It occupies most of your thinking, preventing you from expanding your mind and thinking about other more empowering and important things, doesn't it? You are only able to focus on surviving.

Now think about a route that you are very familiar with, that you may drive daily. It could be from home to work or vice versa. It could be to your friend's house, or to your gym or the local supermarket. What do you focus on while driving? While of course you are focusing on driving safely, you could be thinking about what you're going to do on the weekend, the conversations you will have or the exciting holiday you have coming up.

Your mind is free to think about and focus on anything else that you choose, because you feel safe with familiarity and have certainty that you can achieve your desired outcome. Now, let's apply the uncertainty of not knowing where you are going. Think about when you are driving to a destination you have never been before, maybe to a health appointment or a new restaurant you've been told about and you have no satellite navigation system or anyone to tell you where you're going. Where is your focus then? What are you thinking about?

Isn't your focus wholly and solely on thinking about finding the destination? You want to find the certainty of knowing how to get to the destination as quickly as possible. And until you feel safe with certainty about how to get there and what it looks like, you're unable to think about or focus on anything else.

It's the same for your team when they come to work. If your team don't feel safe with certainty in the working environment, then they can only focus on surviving. If they feel safe and certain within the environment then their mind is free to focus on other more empowering things like achieving their goals and being productive. Structure is another word for certainty or safety in the working world. Let's look at how humans work in relation to certainty, which will give you a bit of an insight into why this is so important.

According to Anthony Robbins (leading life coach, self-help author and motivational speaker), human beings have 6 core needs that should be met to achieve a level of happiness. They are:

- Connection and Significance.
- Certainty and Variety.
- Growth and Contribution.

We will go into more detail about this model later in the book, however for the purpose of understanding why structure is so important, I'm going to summarise it for you.

These six core needs are vital for any and every human being, regardless of who they are or where they find themselves in the world, in order to achieve happiness. The first four are physical needs which, to achieve any level of happiness, we must achieve all four. The last two are spiritual and determine the degree or level of happiness we experience. As humans, we can either meet these needs in a resourceful way, or in a resourceless way. Resourceful means that it's good for us, good for others and good for the greater good. Resourceless means that it's either bad for us, bad for others and/or bad for the greater community.

Certainty is the first of the four physical core human needs in this model, arguably it is also the most sought after. Whether it's met resourcefully or resourcelessly will determine our results either positively or negatively. Certainty is simply understood as establishing some sort of order and control, where its main function is to achieve some level of safety and security.

This is where your leadership comes in. Knowing and understanding that every single human being has a need for certainty or safety means that we must provide a level of certainty in our business for our people to feel safe and be able to focus on achieving the task at hand and ultimately becoming productive and successful.

If we don't meet the need of certainty for our people, they will go about meeting it for themselves and will more likely do so in an resourceless way. For example: Meeting the need for certainty resourcelessly could play out through taking control of their own experience of work. This could be as simple as, 'Well, I don't care what happens anyway, so they can't hurt me' attitude. This gives them certainty that they can control how they don't feel anything for work or their experience at work. Or they could be the 'disrupter' where they gain their certainty through playing the 'funny guy' and disrupting others, gaining their certainty through knowing they will get laughs from their colleagues.

Regardless of what the behaviour is, resourcelessly meeting the need for certainty will always lead to a lack of productivity, preventing the results we are looking for. While people are focused on meeting their need for certainty, they are merely in 'survival' mode. Like in our driving example, they can't focus on anything else until they have this need for certainty met on a consistent basis. The more structure you can provide in your business, the more you will meet their need for certainty and the safer they will feel, enabling them to shift their entire focus to performance. The fewer surprises they experience, the better.

Therefore as leaders, we want to make sure we are helping our people to meet their need for certainty in a resourceful and productive way whilst they are working in our business. There are a number of ways you can do this and as I said, we will get into this in more detail in chapter 10, under the section: *Understanding Human Desires.* However the point to remember is that people want to know what to expect when they come to work, they want advance notice of scheduled meetings and what's expected of them.

As we've discussed in previous chapters, giving your people clear expectations is the foundation to providing them with certainty and safety. These expectations tell them exactly what they need to do and how to behave to be successful. They then have the choice. To ensure that your people are clear, understand and can review them as necessary, have them on display, somewhere away from customers, so they can make an easy reference if need be.

Your daily and weekly meetings are another way to meet the need for certainty. Set a day when you hold a specific meeting each week. For example: if you must have a customer service meeting, then select a day of the week that is suitable for this meeting and communicate it with your team. This gives the team certainty that every Tuesday at 8 am you have your customer service meeting.

Now the content of that meeting will change and vary, depending on results, urgency and performance in this area, which will meet their need for variety. However, the subject of the meeting (e.g. customer service) is the same every Tuesday. You can do this with every subject that you need to discuss as a team each week, giving you a very clear and set meeting structure.

The other common uncertainty people experience in the work environment is their review dates. This can cause all sorts of anxiety and fear in a team member, so the more structured and disciplined you can be around holding these reviews on the same day of the week/month/quarter, the more certainty you will give them. Structure must be tailored to suit the business you are in, so we will look at how to implement a solid structure in detail in chapter 11, giving your people a sense of certainty and safety, freeing their mind to focus on performing.

Chapter 8:
How To Be Disciplined

"With self-discipline most anything is possible."

~ Theodore Roosevelt

Like anything we do, there is a strategy to do it. To brush your teeth successfully, there is a strategy; to drive to work, there is a strategy; to cook dinner, there is a strategy. There is a way to do everything we do either successfully or unsuccessfully. If we find that we're not succeeding at something, all we need to do is to look at the strategy we are using and adjust accordingly. The best way to do this is to find someone who is already achieving what it is you want to achieve.

So, when it comes to discipline, it's no different. There is a strategy to be successful at discipline and there is a strategy to be unsuccessful at discipline. It's not that some people are born with good discipline and others aren't. It is simply that some people have learned, established or discovered a great strategy to achieve successful discipline and others haven't yet.

In this chapter, we will explore what it is we must do to have a successful discipline strategy. These are some of the key actions I took to become a disciplined leader.

- Leading with courage not fear.
- Leading by example.
- Holding your people accountable.
- Follow up or foul up.

Leading With Courage, Not Fear!

Your people want to be inspired. They want to follow a fearless leader, a leader who demonstrates vision, passion, commitment, standards and discipline. A leader who will ensure that the right things are done and things are done the right way. Even if this means putting a few people offside or not being the popular leader. People want to follow a leader who is more committed to the cause than to being liked for making the popular decisions.

If a leader is concerned about upsetting people and worried that they will leave, then this will reduce the standards and the performance of their team. They may be fearful, that if they hold them accountable and expect a certain standard, that the team member/s will be unhappy or unproductive or worse still, resign. This is a common trap that some leaders fall into and, therefore, begin leading with fear.

Leading with a fear of losing people breeds negativity because you hold them to no standard or expectation, which means they do whatever they feel like at the time. We've explored a number of times throughout this book that people will take the shortest and easiest route possible, given the opportunity. More often than not, it's not the same route that will get them the results you or they desire.

Fearing the resignation of a team member holds you ransom to their standard. If they had an acceptable standard, then they would be the leader, not you. So, it's your job to set and maintain the standard of work that is going to lead them, you and your business to the desired outcome you're looking for. If you continue leading with fear, the environment will become so negative as a result of having low expectations that eventually they will choose to leave on their own accord, unhappy with the company and, most likely, unhappy with you as a leader also!

It's like having a personal trainer. Would you prefer a personal trainer who makes everything comfortable for you and easy, and you walk away feeling like you've done nothing at all, or a personal trainer where they push you so hard, you feel muscles you never knew you had? The leader pushes their people to achieve things they didn't believe they could. That's holding them to a high standard. I learned this lesson the hard way, it wasn't a fun experience and I had little success due to leading with fear.

As I stated at the beginning of this book, I'd had some great success in the first two businesses I ran and to expand my experience I moved into a city business. I moved into a team that wasn't making money, even though they had quite a bit of experience between them. When I arrived, I started with what I knew worked. We created a strong vision as a team that was going to see an amazing turnaround. I put in place minimum expectations and all the structure I knew was necessary to make the team successful. I was working my guts out, but nothing was changing.

Have you ever worked so hard yet nothing was working? I gave my all to this team, but for some reason there was a constant negative vibe from them. Regardless of what I was doing, whether it was the weekly business meeting or mini focus meeting, there was always an undertone of negativity. It was something like, "That's not going to work," or, "I'm owed," or, "I'm not working that hard for a massive company, what do I get?" Now, don't get me wrong, individually these guys were lovely people, but they were too jaded in their attitude and had gone way past the point of no return to refocus and become successful.

They had been in an environment where there were no standards. The previous leader had let them do whatever they wanted to, so when I arrived, they weren't interested in meeting any level of expectation. They just wanted to do what they had been doing, which was very little, hence the lack of results.

I knew that these people needed to move on, but given external influences, I was unable to make that happen. These people had been in an environment of low expectations for such a long time, because the leader was fearful of losing them. I arrived and found myself at the end of the equation.

No Expectation + No Support = Poor Attitude and Poor Results

To allow this negative environment to continue is to kiss goodbye your success as a leader, and I almost did!! You will never make a business successful with a negative undertone like this. One of the biggest lessons I learned in this business was that you can work your hardest to give them all the support they need and provide the right environment. But no matter how much you want it for them and how hard you work to make them successful, if *they* don't want it and *they* aren't prepared to work for it, then they will NEVER be successful. You will go to the grave trying!!

As a leader, we understand the fact that nobody is owed anything!!! No one person is bigger than the whole. If your team members bitch and moan and complain about everything, they will NEVER be successful. If they appreciate what they have and the opportunities thrown their way, then they will have more of those opportunities. If they work hard, they will be successful. If they wait for it to be handed on a platter they will NEVER be successful. THAT IS LIFE!!!

So your job as a leader is to provide the environment where they can work to achieve as much success as they want. You do this by having high expectations and providing a high level of support. High expectations are what you would expect of yourself. How would/do you do their job? Given that you're the leader, imagine your performance level is 100%. Your expectations must be that they meet 100%.

Now, between you and me, they probably won't, they will most likely only hit 80% of what you do. 100% is doing it as you would in every area of their job all of the time. This is simply not realistic most of the time. However, you never communicate that to them, because if they know you only expect 80% then you will only get 60%. So knowing that they'll hit 80% of whatever you do because you expect 100%, means that you must be disciplined and absolutely acknowledge when they miss that 20% performance every time.

To provide a highly-supportive environment, you must have an in-depth training schedule for your team members. When they begin, meet with them weekly for the first 90 days to check in with their progress and that they are receiving the support and help they require. Implementing a 'buddy system' for the first 3 months is also a great idea so they have one person (not always you) to go to, should they need extra help.

After their first 90 days, you can begin to hold them accountable to the high expectations you have in place. Should a team member, after their first 90 days, fall below your expectation, then this is when you apply the tough conversation model (see Chapter 6, *How To Have Tough Conversations*). To remind you, the tough conversation model begins with clarifying their understanding, or lack thereof, in a coaching conversation. Secondly you approach them with a more stern approach, thirdly you hold an official private meeting, and finally, let them know their position is under threat. In the first and second stages, you are clarifying their understanding of the expectations and offering to teach them again if they need it.

This is called leading with courage. Communicate clear expectations and hold them accountable to those expectations, offer support when they need it and consequences when they don't meet those expectations. This way, your environment will be protected from negative attitudes and underperformance.

I have often said, "Protect your environment like it was your mother. Do not let anyone jeopardise it, harm it or destroy it."

If someone does threaten your environment, you must take action to get them to either step up and improve in attitude and/or behaviour, or remove them from the business. This doesn't mean they are a 'bad' person, it just means they may not be a match for the team, business or environment at the time. They most likely will not be aware of this and it's your job as the leader to recognise this early in the piece, rather than letting it get worse, because then nobody is happy.

I have always maintained that you are better off having a team full of inexperienced people who want to be there and want to be successful, than a bunch of experienced and negative team members who can't be bothered. I have witnessed and lead numerous successful businesses that have a team full of inexperienced people and achieved their goals. Vice versa, I have witnessed plenty of examples of experienced teams losing money and not achieving their goals because they have low expectations, low levels of support and subsequently a poor attitude.

Whilst it would also make sense to have this section under the "Environment" chapters, it's under discipline for a reason. To lead with courage requires great discipline from you as the leader. It requires you to address poor performance and poor attitude EVERY time it occurs. This requires your discipline. If you do this thoroughly, then you will set your environment up for success.

ACTIVITY:

Assess your discipline and then your team environment:

On a scale of 1 to 10, 1 being "no standards, low support" and 10 being "clear high expectations, high support with consistent consequences," where would you rate your discipline right now? _____

For each of your team members, what is their attitude towards the company and achieving success? 1 being "poor attitude and underperforming" and 10 being "great attitude and high performer."

Name:	Score:	Name:	Score:
_____	_____	_____	_____
_____	_____	_____	_____
_____	_____	_____	_____
_____	_____	_____	_____
_____	_____	_____	_____

What do you need to do to get your environment to a 10?

_____

_____

_____

Who needs to step up in attitude or behaviour?

_____

_____

_____

Have you recognized any team members who have passed the point of no return and need to be removed from the business?

_____

_____

_____

Leading By Example

Do you have a favourite elite athlete? Is there someone in the sporting world who inspires you? You admire their tenacity, determination and the way they conduct themselves both on and off the field, for example. They may have come from a background of hardship, overcome challenging circumstances to achieve, to become the best of the best. They may have defied all odds, battled and demonstrated sheer determination and persistence to get to where they are today. They may also be a person of integrity, they appear to be a quality person with solid values and beliefs and are a great role model to the youth of today. Whilst they may be few and far between, these people do exist and it's a real pleasure to observe them and share in the celebration of their success. They are confident and are clear on who they are and what they stand for.

On the other hand, have you ever heard a story on the news, of an elite athlete who has an emotional outburst or demonstrates some sort of anti-social behaviour, whether it be drinking, fighting or even adultery. These people are meant to be role models for the younger generations and when you hear them speak professionally, they share their stories of hard work and determination, overcoming adversity to achieve and be the best, which is inspiring. Yet their negative behaviour leaves a bad taste in your mouth, leaving you disappointed in them and possibly even resulting in a loss of respect for them.

Which of these two sports people would you hold a greater respect for? Unless you admire anti-social behaviour, I'm going to assume that it's the first description, a sports person who conducts themselves with integrity, honesty and a desire to be the best version of them that they can possibly be.

Have you ever worked for someone who has said one thing and done another? They have one set of rules for themselves and another set of rules for everyone else. I remember very clearly how I felt when I was on the receiving end of this approach, and it wasn't pleasant. Whether you've experienced it or not, I'm sure you can imagine this kind of leadership style. "Do as I say not as I do" is quite frustrating and uninspiring. The fastest way to lose credibility as a leader is to reprimand someone for something that you do.

Remember back to the beginning of this book when we talked about the *Be, Do, Have* model? This is where the rubber hits the road. Demonstrating who we expect our people to be is the most authentic and effective way of leading. It's very simple. Be the attitude, the energy, the emotion that you expect your people to be. Do all behaviour, expectations, customer service, administration and boring jobs as you expect your team to do.

As a leader, you are teaching your people all day everyday how to behave, whether you are aware of it or not. A part of becoming a leader is accepting and understanding that you are under the microscope continually, all day every day. Your people are watching your every move. It really is pretty simple: do as you expect your team to do. If you find through doing, that an expectation is unrealistic or unachievable, then you know you must review it and change it for everyone. Otherwise, do everything that is on your minimum expectations list every single time.

This requires you to have discipline. However, I found it's easier to have discipline and do as you expect of others than it is to lead a demotivated team disillusioned as a result of a 'do as I say, not as I do' leadership style. This includes everything from meeting your expectations to admitting if you make a mistake (we're all human) by addressing it with the team, acknowledging it and apologising (if you'd expect an apology from them).

A challenge that I commonly experienced in the past was being on time, this isn't a good start when you're a leader, with the intention to lead by example. Most of the time I would work around this challenge and arrive on time. However, on the odd occasion when I would be late, I would say something along the lines of, "I'd like to apologise for my tardiness this morning, I'll really put in an extra effort to ensure this doesn't happen again." Whilst it was uncomfortable to do this, I knew that if I expected an apology from a team member who was late, then I had to demonstrate this first.

The most difficult part of this was that given that I had 'done' this behaviour, I could NEVER address lateness with a team member with my integrity intact. To do so would be hypocritical. Thankfully they were mostly good at being on time. If there was a team member who also struggled with being on time, there were two ways I could approach it:

Firstly, I had the understanding of the challenge, as it was also mine, so could share some strategies that I use to help in this instance.

Secondly, I could have established an arrangement where we kept each other accountable to being on time or even create a competition, where the first person who's late loses and has to buy the other a coffee.

This would let your team member know that it's not acceptable to be late, however prevent the negative feeling of a 'you can't tell me off, because you do it' attitude. It keeps it light and removes the 'dictatorship' energy. You will also feel more authentic as a leader as you'll be maintaining your integrity.

The other thing that's important to note here is that what's important to you, isn't necessarily important to others. Being aware of this is essential and as you grow and evolve as a team, you'll come to learn what the 'non-negotiables' are for each team member. In the example above, because my team worked so incredibly hard all of the time, it wasn't that important to me if they were a couple of minutes late. However, I had other team members who felt that if someone in the team was late it meant they didn't respect the rest of the team. These are two opposing perspectives, and both totally valid and reasonable. It is for that reason that it's really important to be clear on what the 'non negotiables' are for all in the team and communicate them in your expectations.

Holding Your People Accountable

Your ability to hold your people accountable is a vital skill in your leadership tool kit and is essential if you are to achieve any level of success.

Think about your car. Isn't a car a vehicle that gets you from where you are now to where you want to be in the future? If one of the parts in your car doesn't function properly or stops doing its job then it will either break down or become more expensive to run, which, if left long enough, will eventually prevent you from moving forward. If you were driving the car and something malfunctioned and slowed the car down or started to make funny noises, then you would address that issue, wouldn't you? Or would you? Isn't it also true that sometimes, depending on which part it is, you can ignore the clanging sound or the red light for a period of time? I certainly have been known to do this in the past. However, we all know that the longer you leave it and ignore the clanging sound or the red light, the worse the problem is going to get and the more expensive it is going to be to fix.

Now imagine that the team that you're leading is like a car. So your team is the vehicle to get you from where you are now to where you want to be in the future, and you are the driver of that car. Your only job as the leader is to ensure that the 'vehicle' is functioning at its optimal level all of the time to ensure that it gets you from A to B as efficiently and effectively as possible.

This is much easier said than done and is the constant and everlasting challenge of leadership. Why?? Because the vehicle, so to speak, is made up of human beings and humans have their own feelings, desires, their own thought processes, life experiences, beliefs, values and habits, just to name a few variables. The key for you as the leader is to know how to get the very best out of each individual. This is what we have been building towards in this book, understanding what makes people tick, how to be the best leader you can be, and how to communicate in a way that motivates and drives them.

Here is where we can expect to begin seeing results. You have established a clear vision, set goals and determined your strategies (we'll get to that part in the coming chapters), set out and communicated your clear expectations, and are about to introduce and follow a simple structure. If you are leading by example, as a demonstration, then there is absolutely no reason why the right team members cannot perform.

Now a distinction we must make here, is the difference between the people in your team and their behaviours. Whilst looking at the team as a vehicle can seem a little mechanical, it's helpful to understand this next point. When one of the parts of the vehicle breaks down or isn't working properly, the first step you take is to see how you can fix the behaviour of that part. It's not necessarily the part itself that is the problem, it's the way it's working. You don't go and replace the whole engine when there is a clanging sound, you look to rectify the problem first. So you must set about correcting the way the engine is working. Once you have done this and it begins working properly again, you have a well-functioning vehicle again.

It's the same with leadership. If one of your team members stops working or functioning properly, you must address the way they are working. It's not necessarily the person that is the problem at this stage, it's their behaviour.

I know this may seem like the same thing, but it's an extremely important distinction for you to make. Your people are not their behaviours. I'll say it again – *your people are not their behaviours*. So when something goes wrong, or they choose a bad attitude for a moment, reprimand the behaviour, not the person. Once you have addressed the behaviour and they resume doing their job well, then you as the leader have done your job. Should the part, or the person, continue to not do their job, then after addressing the behaviour, and attempting to correct the dysfunction, you would proceed to replace the part of the engine that isn't working or the person in your team who isn't working. If you think of accountability in this way, then it makes it a very clear-cut process. So then the question remains, how do you ensure that you are holding your people accountable?

Well it's quite simple. If they do not meet the minimum expectations that have been set and agreed to by the whole team, then it must be addressed. As a leader you have a choice here: you can, like I have in the past, ignore the first little 'sounds' or the 'flashing red light', but I promise you, the longer you leave it, the worse the problem will get.

I highly recommend addressing any offence against your minimum expectations, no matter how small or unimportant it may appear. In the beginning, you may well be constantly addressing breaches of your minimum expectations all the time, however as time passes and your team see that you mean business, they will learn that they must do their job correctly the first time round. This is what creates a 'high expectations' environment. Whilst it might feel like you are nit-picking and seem quite confrontational, I assure you, it's much less confrontational than what lies ahead if you ignore it.

What this does is it communicates a high level of expectation and standard to your team and anything less will not be tolerated. The best part about this is that when they operate in this way, they will be more successful themselves and will begin to appreciate your level of discipline.

For more detail around the conversation to have to address these issues, go back and read the section under chapter 6, *How To Have Tough Conversations*. To refresh your memory:

FIRST TIME:

"The Coaching Conversation" – ensure they understand the minimum expectations around the specific issue' and re-teach any area they appear to be uncertain about.

SECOND TIME: (Same scenario)

Remind them of your original conversation and begin to use more stern language. Check in again with their level of understanding around the minimum expectations in relation to this specific issue.

THIRD TIME:

"Private Official Meeting" – Remove them from their usual work environment for an official meeting. Ensure that you document everything that is discussed and agreed. Continue with firm language.

FOURTH TIME:

Repeat third time and add at the end:

"Should this happen again, your position in this team will be questioned and official performance management will begin."

Ensure that your notes are documented clearly with a specific action plan.

*Remember to check with your local workplace standard legalities when it comes to performance management.

Follow Up or Foul Up

What comes first, the chicken or the egg? It's a commonly known question, yet always an unclear answer with room for debate on both sides. It's the same with leadership. What comes first, being disciplined or follow up? Are you a disciplined leader because you follow up, or do you follow up because you are a disciplined leader? Regardless of which side of the fence you sit, follow up is an important aspect of discipline in leadership.

A leader may have the greatest meetings and performance reviews, with the most inspiring action plans, however regardless of what is discussed and agreed upon in a meeting, if it's not followed up then it will bear little impact on the results of the individual or team.

The Oxford Dictionary states that follow up is 'a continuation or repetition of something that has already been started or done.' This can be in relation to anything in business, it may be the minutes of a meeting, a performance review or performance management, it may be whilst dealing with a customer complaint or a staffing issue. Regardless of the context of the situation, the act of following up is what will ensure that what needs to be done, gets done by all parties involved.

As I've mentioned many times before, people will take the short-cut to get to the end of a task, which could mean they won't do it at all. The challenge with leading is that you are relying on other people to do their job and do it well. The more they know you will check in with them to see how they are going, expect updates and want to be advised when it's completed, the more likely they will, firstly complete it, and do so thoroughly.

The best way to ensure that you follow up what needs to be done is to ensure that it's written down. Whether that be in the meeting minutes, in the performance review document, in your diary or on your to-do list. Get into the habit of writing everything down in one central document and ensure that you operate from and review that document multiple times per day. The best format I've found is by using a diary with dates on it. Then you can document required follow up for the future, as agreed upon by the team or individual. When you become a leader who follows up and holds people accountable, they will miraculously begin to do their work efficiently the first time. It's almost like magic.

> To download your complimentary step-by-step system on 'How to hold your team accountable', simply go to www.leadershipskillsreducethebills.com

PART 4
Environment

Chapter 9:
The Recipe to
a Motivational
Environment

"Business is a subset of environment, not the other way around. You can't have a healthy economy, you can't have a healthy anything in a degraded environment."

~ Peter Coyote

As we'll discover in more detail, the leader of the team or business has the biggest influence over the quality of the environment. If they are generally happy and positive, they will potentially create a happy and positive environment. If they are consistently negative and angry, they will struggle to create a positive environment. Therefore, the degree of awareness the leader has about themselves and the environment around them will determine the degree to which they consciously choose the environment they create.

We will begin exploring how to create a positive and empowered environment with who we need to *be* as a leader and gain further insight into how we operate as humans.

We'll do this by looking at:

1. Why is your environment so important anyway?
2. The power of your intention.
3. The importance of consistency.
4. The art of leadership relationships.
5. The benefits of a powerful leadership team.

Once we've explored the understanding of who we need to be, then we'll move into what actions we must take to create the desired environment.

How Important Is Your Environment Anyway?

A fruit tree grows when it has rich soil and plenty of water to nourish it. When it experiences a nutrient-rich environment consistently for the period of its life span, it will bear much fruit many seasons over. If you plant a fruit tree in the desert to grow in sand with little or no water, it will struggle to survive and therefore be unable to repay you with any fruit. In fact, there are very few trees or plants that can survive healthily in this environment. Isn't it also true that when you plant the fruit tree, you must love and nurture it for many months, if not years, before you see any fruit in return? You don't plant the fruit tree and expect to see fruit instantly, do you?

A leader determines the quality of the environment in any business or team. The leader is like the nutrients in the above example. The quality of the nutrients will determine the health of the fruit tree which will then determine the condition of the fruit. The quality of the leadership will determine the health of the environment and the productivity and success of the team. If the leader provides a nourishing and supportive environment in the infancy of the team, the people will learn and grow, providing the leader with the 'fruit' of success for many seasons in return. As a wise woman once shared with me, "There is a time to sow and a time to reap, and it doesn't happen in the same season." Providing a supportive environment doesn't give you instant results, like a fruit tree doesn't bear fruit instantly. Given that you understand that there is a time to sow, and then there is a time to reap, you can trust that the results will come if you are consistent.

The quality of the environment you provide for your team is crucial to your success. Whether you are aware of it or not, when people walk into your business/team environment, they can feel whether it's a positive or negative environment. The clue as to what the environment is like begins with how the team members interact with each other, how they talk to each other, ask questions, answer questions, their body language and the tone of voice they use, just to name a few. The quality of the environment will determine the long-term results of your team/business and will determine how successful you are as a leader.

I like to describe the environment as the 'overall feeling of the team'. The official definition of an environment is "the surroundings or conditions in which a person, animal, or plant lives or operates." It's important to understand that the environment is fluid and by that I mean it's forever changing and evolving. This is why being a consistent leader is crucial to your success because it can take a long time to build a solid and positive environment, however, it can very rapidly deteriorate from just one mishandled situation.

It's like trust in a relationship. When you begin a relationship, you have the opportunity to continue building on that trust with a nice clean foundation. If you break that trust, then you have to work twice or maybe even three times as hard, and you still may never return it to its original state. You have the best opportunity to have a positive environment when you first start as a leader in your team/business. You can either keep the positive environment by applying all that you are learning through valuing your people, or lose the positive environment by going against all that you've learned by disrespecting them. If that happens, then you will have to work twice or even three times as hard to get it back, and even then, there's no guarantee that you will earn back the trust of your people.

I have been known to say that you must protect your environment like it was your mother. You must adopt the attitude that no one messes with your environment, and anyone that tries will be dealt with immediately. It's that feisty and fiery feeling in your belly, that you have worked so hard to build it and you will prohibit anyone from interfering with it – not a team member, not a competitor, not even a customer.

So let's get to work on saving you a whole heap of heartache, hard work and frustration, and look at how to establish and maintain a healthy and supportive environment so you can continue to provide a positive and empowering workplace.

Your Intention

Although we have discussed the concept of intention in detail previously, it's extremely important that we acknowledge its importance in the Environment section of this book as it's what will ultimately determine what kind of environment you create.

The quality of your environment begins with your intention as a leader. So go back and review your intention that you chose in chapter 5 and ask yourself, "Does this intention help me create the kind of environment I'm looking to create?" Many people experience life by just existing, they don't achieve what they would like to and are generally more miserable than they are happy. A big part of the reason for this is that they have no intention for what they want. They haven't taken the time to get clear on what they want to achieve, so have no idea where they're heading in life. They are usually, however, very clear on what it is they don't want, and could talk about all the things they dislike and don't want in their life, which is probably exactly what they are currently getting.

As I mentioned previously, the definition of intention is "a thing intended; an aim or plan." It is knowing what your desired outcome is in the situation at hand and then adjusting your behaviour accordingly. If you are a leader and have an intention to 'serve and support my people with a servant's heart to help them improve', then your communication, your actions and who you're being would demonstrate a sheer desire to help them improve. Regardless of the situation, it will give them the opportunity to learn and walk away from each interaction with you feeling empowered and knowing exactly what they need to do.

Compare this with having no intention and no consideration of how your team experiences the environment. Your communications, your actions and who you are being on a daily basis will vary and change depending on what mood you're in, which means you'll be inconsistent on every level. This means you are untrustworthy and are providing a lack of certainty or safety in your environment, which causes a 'survival' mentality rather than a 'successful' mentality.

Regardless of what it is – your overall intention as a leader, a conversation, a meeting or working with a customer – if you don't set a clear intention, then you could end up just going round and round in circles, wasting everyone's time, leading to all parties involved becoming frustrated and disengaged. It's like getting into the car and just driving. You don't know where you are going to end up and you certainly don't hit the destination that you were meant to hit.

A great way to set an intention is to think in pictures. What does the desired outcome look like? How do you look after having achieved this desired outcome? How do people look and feel around you? By picturing the outcome as you desire, it will help you get clearer on what your intention is. You can practise this with a conversation you need to have with a team member in the future and build until you can picture your intention as a leader.

Visualising Your Intention:

1. Fast forward in your mind to the time when this situation/conversation/desire is achieved or over.
2. Think about and picture what the desired outcome looks like. How do you feel when the outcome you desire eventuates?
3. Put into words who you had to *be* and what you would like the other person/people to walk away knowing, thinking and feeling.

The first half of the sentence is around who you were 'being' and the second half of the sentence is about what the other person will get out of it. For example: "My intention is to be present and patient with this person when communicating how to achieve my expectation, enabling them to walk away with the knowledge and confidence to apply their new learning."

Like we discussed back in chapter 5, you can use this style of intention setting for a variety of different contexts. In addition to your intention, you can set your intention this way for a heavy duty meeting you have to lead, a customer complaint conversation or a performance management conversation.

This style of intention setting is extremely powerful because your unconscious mind cannot differentiate between what's imagined and reality, which communicates to your unconscious mind that the event has already happened through visualising it. This, in turn, will attract this outcome to you easily because when the unconscious mind believes that it's already happened, it makes it a lot easier to replicate it a second time round.

The Importance Of Consistency

Have you or someone you know, ever tried to lose weight? Do you know what your goal is when you set out to lose weight? What are you focused on? What are your actions? Possibly you are focused on how many kilos or pounds you want to lose. You are focused on not wanting those jeans to be so tight anymore and not wanting to feel 'fat' any more. Essentially, you may be motivated away from what you don't want.

Like we learned in chapter 7, when you are motivated and focused on what you don't want, the result can only be temporary unless you switch your focus to what it is you do want. Whilst the 'away from' motivation is great to trigger action, if that's the only way you are motivated, then it leads to inconsistent results because once you achieve 'getting away from what you don't want', you'll slip back into the old habits leading right back to where you began, if not worse, because there is no more motivation.

In leadership, consistency is all about being disciplined with the right behaviour all the time. It is about ensuring that your behaviour and expectations are consistent and you will address related issues with team members regardless of who they are.. This will determine the type of environment you provide.

A great way to ensure that you are consistent and fair is to direct your focus on your purpose or desired outcome. Begin each day with a thought or vision of what it is you're wanting to achieve, and what the end goal or desired outcome is. So, like in the example, rather than focusing on what you don't want, e.g. "I don't want to be fat" or "I don't want to lose customers, money or staff", you are focusing on what you do want. "I want to be fit, healthy and full of vitality" or "I am committed to taking a step towards my vision."

There is a motion of your focus. One is away from what you don't want, and the other is towards what you do want. Notice that there is a feeling of heaviness to the 'away from' focus, and almost a lightness to the 'toward' focus. I know this seems really obvious and simple, but it is such a common mistake that people make and has a massive impact on results.

It may sound like an obvious flip; knowing what you don't want means you know what you do want, right? Not necessarily, even if you are clear on what you don't want, to answer the question 'What is it you do want?' can be quite difficult to articulate. So practise focussing on, thinking about and talking about what it is you do want to maintain consistency.

The clue as to whether you are focused away from or towards what you want is the negation in your language or the 'negative' word. So 'don't want' or 'not' or 'won't' are good examples of 'away from' focus/language. If you hear one of the negations come out of your mouth or in your thoughts, or you are getting inconsistent results, then check in with where your focus is and flip it. Ask yourself, "Okay, so what is it I do want?" Be sure to write down the answer, check and recheck your answer to ensure there are no negations in your new focus.

The best way to ensure that you maintain the right focus is to build it into your daily morning routine as you begin work. Do you have a daily focus meeting? Start the meeting every morning talking about the vision and what it means to each of you. You can mix it up so that it doesn't get boring, however on some level, make the beginning of each day a focus on your vision.

As we explored in the last section, another way to ensure you are consistent is to always have a clear intention as a leader. This will help you maintain consistency because it's your intention that will drive who you're 'being' and the actions you take.

The Art Of Leadership Relationships

As a leader, there is such a delicate line between establishing and maintaining a disciplined environment and ensuring there is a fun and supportive atmosphere at the same time. The difference is a productive and positive relationship or an unproductive and destructive relationship with your team. Simply by having an awareness of the fine line will give you the opportunity to create the right relationship with your team.

As leaders, we must gain respect and have the ability to discipline as required, and at the same time, we must be able to let our hair down, have fun with our team, be ourselves and allow them to be themselves also. When a leader manages to establish this fine balance, the team is happy, productive and successful.

Too much authority and discipline could lead to unhappy unproductive and disrespectful team members, and too much fun will also lead to an unproductive and unsuccessful team environment, ultimately leading to an unhappy team. It is, therefore, exceptionally important to learn the art of balancing your leadership relationships on this fine line between discipline and fun.

The Oxford dictionary defines 'relationships' as "the way in which two or more people or things are connected". The way you connect with each team member will determine the quality of your relationship with them. The relationships you have with your team will then determine your ability to lead them successfully.

To connect with your team, you must begin with being authentically you. There's no point trying to be like another leader. I've done it and it doesn't work. I remember when I was appointed as the National Operations Manager, I stepped in to the role and I was replacing a strong and powerful leader. I thought that I had to be exactly like her, so tried to demonstrate the same strength and power. As a result, I forgot who I was and my own strengths, the reason why I was given the position in the first place. Instead, I was inconsistent and unfair, making decisions I thought I should make rather than the decisions I knew were right. All it did was lead to frustration and negativity from the team and poor results.

Your people will see through you faster than a lightning bolt. You are you and nobody else can bring what you can to your team. It's here that you must be good at recognising your strengths, understanding your weaknesses and working with them, to bring out your best as a leader.

There's also no point in trying to make it look like you never make a mistake. You must bare all to your team, warts and all, to be authentically you. The only way to start being authentically you is to lose any ego you operate with, or at least have the awareness of what your ego is. Being driven by your ego means that you are more concerned about yourself than you are about your team. They will pick this up very quickly and lose respect just as fast.

There is no benefit in having an ego as a leader. When you think about it, what is the ego? It's our self-esteem, self-worth or self-confidence, and the need to prove that we are capable and we relate all of this to our ability.

Unfortunately, as humans, we like to have our ego constantly stroked and most of us feel we need to defend our title, our position, our ability, and highlight how good we are in order to feel good enough for the role that we are playing. You know what, you're in a leadership position because someone believes in you and you believe in yourself enough to have this opportunity. You can do this job and you can do it well. If you implement only half of the training in this book, then you will be streets ahead of most leaders out there.

Therefore, there's no benefit in asserting your authority over your team to show them and tell them how good you are. There's also no point in expecting to hear it from your team. It is not the job of your team to stroke your ego, they are too busy worrying about how they are performing to notice you or your performance. It is, however, your job to stroke their ego, because when they feel confident, they are successful. One of the things I can guarantee is that you will do a lot for many, and unfortunately, it can sometimes be a very thankless job from the external world.

So choose to find your ego boost in something other than what people tell you, or what you tell other people. I found it in watching my team succeed, achieving what they had set out to. I knew that I helped them achieve by providing the environment they needed to grow and develop. I loved that, that's what drove me.

Allow yourself to be vulnerable in your team environment and be okay with making mistakes and admitting it. As long as you acknowledge it and correct it, then that's all you must do. This also allows you to be more empathetic to your team, when they make mistakes. There really isn't any other alternative. Some leaders think that by pretending to be perfect, covering up mistakes, not admitting it, that nobody sees it. Guess what, they do, they will and the more you try to cover it up, not admit it and try to appear perfect, the quicker they will lose respect for you as a leader. I wonder if you've ever had an experience with a leader like this? It's pretty common in leadership and it's probably the worst thing you can do.

Your people won't let their guard down and have fun with you unless you are authentically you! When something isn't done correctly, the person concerned must be made aware of this. It's not okay to get frustrated with them behind their back or discuss it with someone else. It is as simple as advising them of what went wrong and then helping them learn/become aware of the right way. This may be a point where you use the "Tough Conversations" script we've discussed previously. The most important point here is that you are honest and clear when you need to give feedback. Ensure that they understand what you've said and what their next step is in order to rectify it.

A great way to ensure they understand is to ask them to clarify what you have told them. Essentially, have them repeat back what they have learned in their own words. Like we discussed in the Listening Skills section of this book, clarification is an important part of communication because it ensures that the meaning of the communication is understood by all involved. It's as simple as repeating back what they've heard to ensure they've understood exactly what you're saying. It prevents unnecessary defensiveness and misunderstandings.

Disciplining when people breach your minimum expectations is essential to managing the fine line of relationships. Whether you are aware of it or not, if you don't discipline the behaviour of breaching the minimum expectations, then everyone else in the team will notice, become frustrated, and may also choose not to meet them. If this continues repeatedly, it will destroy your environment and lead to a team of disengaged and apathetic members.

Regardless of how small the offence is, you must acknowledge it and address it with the individual concerned. This can be as simple as looking at them with a serious face and saying, "Joan, is that what we agreed upon?" if it's minor and first offence, or utilising the 'Tough Conversations' script to address a major or a repeating issue. Either way, if what's meant to be done isn't done, then you must address it.

When your team is performing and meeting all minimum expectations, it's time to have some fun. If you lead this fun, they will think you're amazing! If initiating fun doesn't come naturally to you, then you can diarise it! Fun can be as simple as introducing a 'whoopy cushion' for example, or having a laugh with the team! I introduced a 'frog' at the front door of the shop that would *ribbit* every time someone would walk in. It got laughs from both the customers and the staff!

Value and respect each team member as you want them to value and respect you. This is a simple point but quite a rare quality. As the old saying goes, 'Do unto others as you would have done unto you'. Finally, be the harmonising influence. This means be the problem-solver, not the problem-creator. Whenever a problem arises, calmly address the facts only. Never deal in 'he said, she said' emotional conversations, as you will end up in quicksand, slowly sinking. Simply find out the facts and work a solution from there using the I.G.R.O.W. model.

The Benefits Of A Powerful Leadership Team Chosen On Purpose

The types of leadership styles used when running a team together can significantly impact the results of a business and success of the individuals in that team. It is therefore valuable to understand what your leadership style preference is so you can make an educated guess about the right type of 2IC (Second In Charge) you should have. At a very basic level, it's very clear that there are two distinctive types of leadership styles. There is the:

1.   Leader style.
2.   Manager style.

Both of these leadership styles can produce highly successful business leaders and the sooner you become aware of your preferred style, the sooner you can start utilising your strengths and planning around your weaknesses.

A **Leader** is typically good at all aspects of leadership that relates to the people. This includes, but isn't limited to, the vision, communication, creating a positive environment, inspiring and motivating their people, and running effective meetings.

A **Manager** is typically good at the business side, which includes, but isn't limited to, knowing the numbers of the business, analysing the KPI's to establish how to drive the business forward, thinking ahead to avoid problems in the future and being organised for a seamless structure.

Whilst there is a a lot more detail we could explore around personality profiles and strengths and weaknesses to benefit your leadership ability, here we're just going to skim the surface to give you the awareness of a very broad overview.

In case you haven't clicked, I'm very good at the Leader style. I have always been great at communicating with people and have had to work really hard on my Manager style. I am great with running a fun and motivational environment, I can help people work through challenges with customers or work colleagues, I can sell a great vision and bring energy to the room. This means that I have had to work really hard on knowing my numbers, and looking at the Profit & Loss statement and understanding it.

Another challenge for me was establishing a structure to be organised. As a business leader, it's important to have a 2IC, someone to 'have your back', support you, to confide in and strategize with. My first 2IC was a Manager style. This is the best combination of a leadership team, a Leader style and a Manager style, complimenting each other's strengths. When you are interviewing for your 2IC, if you consider this it will set you up for great success down the track.

I then had a 2IC whose style was Leader, like me. We weren't together long, which is probably a good thing because our financials were up the creek. We did, however, have a lot of fun and some success!!

My third 2IC was a talented individual as he was the first and one of the very few leaders I have worked with who easily adopts both styles, Leader and Manager. This made us a super strong leadership team as we had lots of fun as well as the attention to detail and discipline (thanks to him) to run a very tight ship.

If you are a Manager style, then your opportunity is to improve your communication and the quality of your environment for your people. All the strategies and training in this book will give you a clearer understanding of how to do this.

If you are a Leader style then your opportunity is to work on the tasks/numbers focusing on the detailed aspects of the business. Often you will also need to improve in organisation and preparation for meetings, staff reviews etc.

The best way I found to do this is to create yourself so much structure that it's done for you. The way I did this was to create templates for EVERYTHING. This meant for meetings/ performance reviews we always had an agenda and we documented everything discussed, which meant that I could easily follow up in the next meeting/performance review. You will find these templates and more information about the different leadership styles and how to work with them on my membership website www.leadershipskillsreducethebills.com

ACTIVITY:

Take a moment to reflect on and establish what your natural leadership style is. Do you naturally relate to the Leader Style or the Manager Style? If you feel you are both, then yay for you! Congratulations, you're a rare breed.

Reflect on and establish what your 2IC's natural leadership style is. Do they relate with the Leader or the Manager Style?

_____

Now work out a plan together, to ensure that you're embracing each other's strengths and minimising the effects of your weaknesses.

Chapter 10:
The Sprinkles On Top

*"There are two things people want more than
sex and money... Recognition and praise."*

~ Mary Kay Ash

Like we discussed in the Discipline section, there are strategies that we use to do everything in life that either work for us and get us the results we're looking for, or that don't get us the results we're looking for. Whether we are aware of it or not, as the leader, we are creating the environment of our team and business. We are the single greatest influence on the environment that exists. There are things we can do that will contribute to a great environment and others that will contribute to a poor environment.

Like many things, simply having the awareness that you are creating the environment will give you the ability to change it, however we're going to take a look in more detail around what things you can do, and what you must stop doing, to create a positive and empowered environment. They include:

- Understanding and meeting human desires.
- How the team feels = $$ in your pocket.
- Praise and recognition.
- Team morale.
- Adapting to change successfully.

Once you've completed this chapter, you'll be fully armed with the know-how, to significantly impact your environment in a positive way.

Understanding Human Desires

Have you ever owned a dog? If not, do you know someone who has? As a dog owner, it's important for you to understand there are certain responsibilities that come with owning this dog for its happiness and survival. You must feed them, ensure they've got water, groom them, treat them for fleas, provide shelter, and take them for a walk. It doesn't necessarily matter in which order you do them, as long as you do each of them regularly. If you leave one or two of these out, then it would impact on the dogs happiness and ability to survive. And depending on which ones you leave out, it would also determine the severity of the impact on its happiness and survival.

This understanding is similar to meeting the needs of your people. As a leader, it is important to understand the needs of your people and increase retention by providing an environment where the team feels happy. If you do this successfully, then you'll continue to build on the experience level in your team and increase their productivity.

Whilst we explored in some detail the six core needs in chapter 7, about meeting the need for certainty for our people to feel safe, it's now important that we explore it in more detail in the context of our environment and how to meet all six core needs through the environment we provide.

Anthony Robins established that every human being, regardless of race, religion, nationality or sex, is built with basic needs otherwise known as the 6 Core Human Needs. As a leader, when you understand these, you then know how and what you can do to help your team meet them at work and retain your people, making your business more successful.

They are:

Certainty	v	Variety
Significance	v	Connection
Growth	v	Contribution

The 3 down the left hand column are all about self, and the three down the right hand column are all about others. If you meet the first 4, *Certainty, Variety, Significance* and *Connection*, then the individual will experience happiness. The extent to how much happiness they feel will be determined by how much they meet and experience the last two, *Growth* and *Contribution.*

As I've mentioned previously, you can also meet the above four needs either resourcefully or resourcelessly. Resourcelessly is when it's to the detriment of self, others or to society. For example: taking drugs would give you the certainty of knowing what you'll feel – maybe relief from the pressures of life, as well as meeting the need for variety through the randomness of what could happen when you're high. They make you feel special, as you're not like the rest of your family or friends (usually). They give you the feeling of Significance and you get to hang with other drug takers, fulfilling the need for connection. However, it's not good for you, those around you and definitely not for society.

Resourcefully meeting the need of Certainty would be living a healthy life style with a routine of exercise by training for a sport that you play. Doing 4 or 5 different types of exercise each week would help you meet the need for variety. Meeting Significance resourcefully could entail achieving a goal in your chosen sport that you have worked towards and receiving recognition for it. Spending time with likeminded individuals, whilst playing that sport, will help you meet the need for Connection resourcefully. The key with this is that if any one thing meets 3 or more of these needs, then it becomes an addiction. So the question I hear you asking is, "Okay, so how do I help my people meet these?"

Below are some suggestions but there are many more you could explore:

Certainty	Structure with morning meetings/weekly business meetings same day, same subject, every week.
	Structure with staff reviews. Always happen on the first or second day of the week, month or quarter.
	Consistency in your moods and how you speak with people by being clear on your intention.
	Consistency in how you make your decisions.
Variety	Hold your morning meetings in different locations.
	Buy them coffees or muffins every now and then.
	Change how you approach the same subject each week.
	Change the content of each meeting each week.
Significance	Recognise the individual for something achieved or well done.
	Use them as an example when addressing the whole team.
	Ask a person of influence to call them to congratulate them.
	Text them after hours to tell them how well they are doing.
	Thank them for their hard work.
	Celebrate the small wins they have like achieving a KPI goal.

Connection	Take the team out for dinner or drinks.
	Ask about them and their personal lives, demonstrate care and concern.
	Have light-hearted fun in the office when things are running smoothly.
	Check in regularly to ensure they are keeping up with their work load.

As you can see, Certainty and Variety work against each other, as does Significance and Connection. So whilst the individual is busy focusing on meeting their need for certainty and getting their environment consistent, they are not meeting their need for variety. This has the potential, if left unnoticed, to lead to a feeling of lack of choice, because everything is the same, which will shrink their comfort zone until eventually they're only comfortable in their bedroom, potentially leading them into a state of depression. To break out of this, they may have a sudden urge to do something wildly crazy to meet that need for Variety.

If an individual is constantly focused on standing out from the crowd to express their uniqueness and meet the need for Significance, they may ignore the need for connection, forgetting their colleagues, friends or people they may have spent a lot of time with previously. Should that individual succeed or achieve, they may then go about reconnecting or seeking new people to connect with who have also achieved something similar, to meet the need for connection.

This often happens when people are climbing the corporate ladder, always pushing themselves for more. When they finally get to the top, they look around and there's no one there, and may not have been for a while. So to meet that need, they may then go on to search for a connection through spending time with their team or seeking out other successful business people through networking.

These six core needs are not just for some people, this is for ALL human beings. A great way to remember to ensure you're meeting your teams six core needs is to diarise it until it becomes habit.

CASE STUDY:

Flight Centre Ltd as a company does a great job in providing an environment where they meet all 6 core needs. Here's a few examples.

Certainty: Every month each individual has a target and the consultant can achieve their target if they provide good customer service and help enough people book their dream holiday. It doesn't change.

Variety: Because every day is different. There are never two days the same. There will always be an enquiry about a place that the consultant has never been to, a trip to organise that they have never organised before or a change to make that they've never made before. Even though they go to the same location to work (which is more certainty), what happens each day is different.

Significance: Through reward and recognition, which is one of the company's philosophies. At their monthly celebration night, known as 'buzz nights', at half year and end of year balls, and the jewel in the crown the Global Ball where they fly their top 10% of performers to an exclusive location around the world and put on a party like they're celebrities.

Connection: Flight Centre is renowned for creating life-long friendships. Because the company employs a certain type of individual, people working for this company tend to have a lot in common. Overall, they are a group of like-minded people who love travel, love to have fun and love success. Usually, they are also prepared to work hard to achieve it.

Growth: There is always an opportunity to do more training, to learn something new, like a new destination, or new skills, like leadership or sales training.

Contribution: is one that can easily be forgotten as a company, but is extremely important and one that Flight Centre does really well. They have what's called the "Flight Centre Foundation" which provides support to many charities, giving the staff an opportunity to volunteer two days per year on company time.

How can your team, business or company go about meeting the six core needs of your people?

ACTIVITY:

Record all the ways you currently meet the six core needs of your people, and then brainstorm all the new ways you could potentially meet these 'six core needs' for your people:

How we currently meet these needs:

How we could meet these needs:

CERTAINTY

_____   _____
_____   _____
_____   _____
_____   _____
_____   _____

VARIETY

_____   _____
_____   _____

_____   _____

_____   _____

_____   _____

SIGNIFICANCE

_____   _____

_____   _____

_____   _____

_____   _____

CONNECTION

_____   _____

_____   _____

_____   _____

_____   _____

GROWTH

_____   _____

_____   _____

_____   _____

_____   _____

CONTRIBUTION

_____   _____

_____   _____

_____   _____

_____   _____

How The Team Feels = $$ In Your Pocket!

Some leaders might discount the feelings of their team, conveying a 'This is business, there's no place for feelings here'-type attitude. Whilst this might appear to be strong and leader-like, it couldn't be further from the truth. This type of leader doesn't deserve the privilege of having a team of people follow them, and they probably don't experience that privilege, even if in a leadership role. The crazy thing about this is that when leaders demonstrate this attitude, for all the reasons we've already discussed in this book, the team is unproductive and unsuccessful and therefore, so are they. If these leaders only understood that how the team feels is a direct correlation to the success they do or do not experience. Wouldn't that be a much more heroic thing to understand, because then they would achieve what they're out to get – success!

Leadership is about leading people, and you only get to do that when the people want to follow you. There are not many people who would choose to follow a leader with such an abrupt and dismissive attitude.

Your leadership has a big impact on how your people feel in their role. I still remember how I felt when working for an uninspiring and rather negative leader, and it wasn't pleasant. I am also well aware of how I feel when I'm working for an inspired, focused and driven leader. Think about the leaders you've had in your time. If you've been unfortunate enough to work for an uninspiring leader, how did you feel? What were your results like? What was your loyalty level like? Compare that to working for an inspiring leader who's committed to your success. If you've been fortunate enough to work for this type of leader, how did you feel, what were your results like and how loyal were you?

How you lead will determine how your people feel, and determine their productivity. It's as simple as that, and everything we've discussed in this book so far has been explaining the 'how to' part of being an inspiring and motivational leader.

So when you become frustrated with your team, angry for any reason, wake up on the wrong side of the bed, have an argument with your partner before work, or anything else that puts you in a bad mood, have a think about whether you want your people to make money, or cost money. If you bring this negative energy into work, it will absolutely cost you money in productivity. Always remember that you determine their productivity level by how you walk into work and how you treat them during the day.

I remember sometimes feeling so angry or frustrated with a team member because they had made a mistake that cost a lot of money and I just wanted to make them feel bad. Horrible I know, and I'm not proud of it. However, somehow I made it 'right' in my own mind, because if I feel bad for what has happened, then I'm going to make sure the employee feels bad also. This is an example of really poor leadership and leads to nothing but lack of productivity.

There is always a consequence to our communication and behaviour, whether it be positive or poor, so depending on what consequence we'd like, this should determine our behaviour. If we're happy to tolerate lack of productivity and negativity, then poor behaviour from ourselves would be acceptable. If we're looking for a productive consequence (which I imagine we are) then our communication and behaviour must be delivered positively, in a way where the team member knows what's right or wrong and then knows how to improve.

A strategy I adopted to overcome this poor style of leadership, to hold myself accountable to this, was to imagine that their mother, father or partner was standing next to them as I'm having the conversation. I know that if I imagine their nearest and dearest next to them, then I'm accountable to them for the language and tone I use and, ultimately, how they receive my communication. As long as I'm comfortable for their loved ones to hear how I'm speaking to them, then I know I'm working with the right intention.

It's easy to forget how much influence and impact you have on a team member. Think back to the time, early in your career, when you first started in a job. How did you see your leader? What did you think of them? How important was it to you what they thought of you? Take a moment to reflect on the power this person had in your world.

You are now that person and, while you may not feel like it, they will be looking to you for belief, support and encouragement, as you hoped for from your leader. Whether you received it or not is irrelevant. You are either the leader you are because of or in spite of your previous leaders. You can choose to have a positive influence over your team or be a negative influence. Leadership brings a huge responsibility as you have control over whether someone is happy at work or not, impacting their overall happiness.

BELIEVE IN YOUR PEOPLE:

One of the most powerful things you can do for someone is tell them how much you believe in them and how much you believe they can achieve their 'big goals'. It's very common for people to lack belief in themselves, and they may only ever gain belief in themselves by their direct leader communicating and encouraging them to keep going. The more you can do this, the better. The caveat is, whatever you say must be true.

You shouldn't say it if you don't believe it, that's dishonest. If they haven't got the potential, then you must ask yourself, "What are they doing in that role?" and find them a more suitable one. If you are not a leader who naturally offers encouragement, that's fine, you're not alone. You simply need to create a system to help remind you, like diarising it, or creating a calendar pop-up.

CREATE YOUR OWN BUBBLE FOR SUCCESS:

There are many variables and negative external influences on business. There is always a reason why you can't succeed, as there is always a reason why you can. After you have determined your minimum expectations, your vision, goals and strategies, this is your internal ball, and that's all you allow the team to focus on.

If things go wrong in the external world, keep your eye on the internal ball. This way you're giving your team the best chance to be exempt from it, because you'll know what you're aiming for – the team vision. If you cultivate an attitude of focusing only on the internal ball, nothing will stop us and sheer determination, then your team will know what they stand for and what they need to do to achieve in any external environment.

I created this attitude with each of my teams, and we never took our eye off what we wanted to achieve, regardless of what was going on around us. I call that the "Bubble of Success". We experienced many highs and lows in the travel industry like 9/11, the collapse of a major airline in Australia in that same week and also the Bali bombings, just to name a few. The one that stands out for me the most, is when I was the National Operations Manager. We were so driven and focused that even through the 'Global Financial Crisis' we doubled the turnover year on year selling something that could be perceived as luxury or unnecessary items – Life Coaching courses.

PRAISE, APPRECIATION AND RECOGNITION:

As I was thinking up examples to demonstrate praise, appreciation and recognition, I was trying to come up with universal experiences or situations where someone would

ALWAYS demonstrate praise, appreciation and/or recognition and do something as simple as say, "Thank you," in a situation. I thought of offering your seat to a pregnant lady, or elderly person on a bus or a train. Sadly, while the majority of times you would probably be thanked, there's always a possibility that you won't be. What about when you hold the door open for someone? Same thing again, more than likely you would be thanked, but I wouldn't want to bet my house on it. What about when you cook dinner for someone? You put your hard work, time and love into cooking a meal, but not always will you be praised or recognised and shown appreciation for what you've done.

That led me to wonder why it is the case. I concluded that sometimes, what we think is the right thing to do, a kind gesture or an achievement, others believe is an expectation or a given that you would do that and therefore doesn't require any acknowledgement.

But think about this: If you were to offer your seat up to 5 different elderly people, and not one of them had said thank you, what would you be inclined to do when you encounter the sixth elderly person? Would you continue to offer your seat? Maybe, however you may also feel less inclined to offer your seat, because it hasn't been appreciated or recognised in the past. This is human nature. What gets recognised, praised and appreciated promotes more of that behaviour, even if it's just a simple 'thank you' or 'well done'. Think about a time when someone has said thank you or well done to you for something you may have done, big or small. How does it make you feel? It can make you feel good about yourself and build your confidence. When you praise, appreciate or recognise someone else, you also gain, as it can set your day positively because you have put a smile on someone's face and helped to build their confidence.

Praising, appreciating or recognising someone can be as simple as acknowledging them by saying, "Thank you, I really appreciate your work on that." Or, "Great job, you have really excelled this time, well done." But, for some reason we may treat these statements like it costs us a fortune every time we say it. When we understand the power of saying thank you, or well done, we are beginning to understand what it takes to be an inspiring leader.

To some people, it may seem pretty simple to show your appreciation or praise, but in the day-to-day busyness of life and work, it could be the last thing on our mind. With the pressure of performance and productivity, we can forget to show the appreciation that we do feel because we take it for granted. Yet, if that behaviour disappeared, we'd surely miss it. So if it isn't a habit for you to praise, recognise and appreciate positive behaviour, it doesn't mean you are a bad person, it just means you need to put some strategies in place to ensure that you remind yourself to say thanks every now and again.

This isn't to say that you say thanks or well done to people for just doing their job all the time, because if you do, the power of it will be weakened, but every now and again doesn't hurt. The more time you take to stop and really be present when saying thank you, the more powerful it will be.

If you need reminding, then make a note in your diary, or a pop-up in your calendar to look for things to say thank you for. When you begin to look for things to recognise or be thankful for, you will start to see more and more things to praise. Like the elderly person on the bus or train, if they were to say thank you, you'd be more inclined to offer your seat again next time. The same goes for the people in your team. When you say thank you or well done, they will be more inclined to demonstrate that behaviour again.

Like we explored in the *Appreciation* section in chapter 5, it can be as simple as saying, "Thank you for doing that report," or it can be a deeper recognition where you acknowledge not only the behaviour they have done, but also the characteristic they possess to have done that. For example: "Thank you for doing that statement, but what I really appreciate is the initiative you've shown to get it done so quickly. Thank you." The behaviour is 'doing the statement' and the characteristic is the 'initiative'.

Another example would be if a team member decided to stay back after work to complete something. A simple, "Thank you for staying back to get that done," would be lovely. And, "Thank you for staying back after work to get that done. I want to let you know that I really admire and appreciate your commitment to your job. Thank you." This would be a more sincere and powerful way to recognise your team member.

The other thing to think about when you're praising or recognising is how you are doing it. Are you doing it one-on-one or in front of the team? It's important to know whether the person you're recognising likes being recognised in public or private. Some people dislike being the centre of attention, and this could work against the intention you have of making them feel good about what they have done. Others absolutely love it and love to have the centre stage, and you couldn't thank them enough in this way. It's important to know your team member and what works best for them.

Whilst we are on private or public recognition, an important side note must be made here about reprimanding. The old saying goes praise in public and reprimand in private. Whilst it's okay to acknowledge and praise in public, it's never okay to reprimand in public. Embarrassing or belittling a team member in public is never okay and will never inspire or motivate your team member to do better. So I'm going to keep it simple. Just never do it. When you're reprimanding, you must do it one-on-

one, so you can ensure understanding and assist them gain the learning to know how to improve for next time. Go back to the *Accountability* section in chapter 8 for more details.

You can also demonstrate praise and recognition through monetary reward. Remember, if you offer a financial incentive, like a voucher or bonus, on a regular basis it may become an expectation and will lose its power. So keep these for when you really need to see some results. The rarer they are, the more powerful they will be.

Team Morale

Can you remember a time when you've walked into a shop or a business and the atmosphere is buzzing, people are laughing, enjoying themselves and there's a really lovely feel to the environment? The staff are communicating well and smiling, you're acknowledged immediately and offered assistance. Doesn't it make you want to stay a bit longer, have a more in-depth look, and ask the questions you have? You're even happy to wait a little longer because you're enjoying the fun environment.

Have you ever walked into a shop or a business and it felt like you could cut the air with a knife? Maybe you notice when the staff communicate with each other, there is a snappy tone and disrespect for each other. They clearly show their frustration or maybe even comment on their thoughts about the other person to you. Or better yet, they roll their eyes after a colleague has spoken to them. Clearly, if any of these situations were present in a team environment, it would be safe to say that there was pretty low team morale in that business.

Team morale is exceptionally important because it is the underlying unseen, but clearly felt, factor that will determine your results. If people feel good emotionally, physically and mentally, then they will be happier, and therefore more productive and efficient at work.

Team morale can be defined as how employees feel about their job, their co-workers, their superiors and the company they work for. It is the overall emotional state that your employees feel on a consistent basis. Great team morale means that everyone is happy and positive and most likely successful. Poor team morale means that the team is unhappy and negative and most likely unsuccessful.

I remember someone telling me that teams that play together, stay together. This means that people are generally happier when there is a social aspect to their working environment. This is especially true for Generation Y, because they typically have grown up in 'broken' families, so they look to find their support structure in other environments, especially at work. The more you can provide a safe, supportive and fun work environment, the more loyal they will be.

I remember when I opened a new business, our results were lacking because we were starting from zero. So I set my team a challenge at every work function, to be the team that was there the latest. In our own minds, we won if this was the case. What happened through doing this was that the morale of the team became stronger and stronger as we built more and funnier memories by spending lots of time together.

There are many things you can do to build your team morale. That example is one way of building team memories and fun stories together, either at work functions or scheduling a team outing once per month or quarter.

On a side note, if there is alcohol involved, then ensure you remain in control. Yes you can drink, but never to the point of obliteration. If you know that you tend to do that when drinking, then discipline yourself. This is not a session with your mates; you are still the leader, even when out on the town.

They will still be watching you and will lose respect if you are totally out of control.

The event doesn't have to be business-funded or organised, and it doesn't have to be expensive. It could be something as simple as a BBQ at someone's house. Bowling, skirmish and ropes courses are also great team outings that build memories and create laughs for the team to talk about while back in the work environment.

Other activities you can do to improve the morale of your team:

- Hold a casual clothes day and raise money for a charity of their choice.
- Hold a morning tea and get everyone to bring a gold coin for a donation.
- Buy the team pizza for lunch.
- Run incentives. Eg: "Best On Ground" team member award for the month, where throughout the month the whole team casts votes by writing a note and putting it in a 'BOG' box. At the end of the month, you get together as a team and read out the votes and then the person with the most votes wins.
- Anything that gets them together and communicating will contribute to the morale of your team.

Another way you can build team morale is to ensure that you know and then recognise and celebrate important dates and events for the team. Whether it be birthdays, anniversaries, or both. Remembering and saying, "Happy Birthday!" or, "Happy Anniversary!" first thing in the morning – or even better, giving them the day off so they can enjoy it with their family – will go a long way to building your team morale. This is because it demonstrates that you care about them as a person and value them as more than just a result at the end of the day. If you forget or don't know, that can retract from all of the hard work you have done to build the team morale because you're communicating that you don't care about them as a person, rather, just a result at the end of the day. One way you can do this, is to put each team members birthday and work anniversary into your phone and set a reminder each year. I did this as a leader of over 100 people, and whilst it took a while to set up, it was exceptionally easy to recognise these milestone dates for my team, which made them feel valued and special.

Smile more, you have the sole power of determining the atmosphere of the working environment. This was my favourite part of being a leader, because it meant that I got to ensure that every day would be a good day. Simply by walking in to work with a smile on my face and a cheery, "Good Morning!" meant that everyone started the day on a positive note. I know it sounds really simple, however it's one of the most powerful things you can do in the morning. This, in turn, will rub off on your team and make them feel happy, even if they weren't when they arrived at work. In coaching, we have a saying that "Physiology creates psychology." If you smile when you're angry, you cannot continue to be angry. Changing your body language will change how you feel.

Value your team members as people. Encourage them to take a break, to leave the office for lunch and get some fresh air. The more you communicate to them that you care for them as a person, the happier they will be at work.

Help your team members achieve goals outside of work. Ask them about their personal goals and reference them as often as you can (we'll explore this in depth later in the book). Help them get out of work on time if they have an appointment after work and demonstrate that you care about their whole life, not just work.

Save 'no' for the big things. If you can say 'yes' when they need to leave an hour early for a medical appointment or something that is important to them, you will get much more productivity out of them in the other 7 or so hours they are there than if you say no and have them there for 8 hours. If you go above and beyond for them, then they will do the same for you.

When you apply what you have learned in this book combined with these key points, you will absolutely have created positive team morale. There are many other things you can do to build team morale. The underpinning key to building morale is to demonstrate that you care about your people as people, rather than just output.

Adapting To Change

It's safe to say that the introduction of the internet was one of the most significant changes in business in the modern era. There were many businesses that existed in the 80s and early 90s that simply don't exist now because they didn't change, evolve and adapt to the new business environment. A good example of this is Borders Books: A major retail book store chain in Australia, which didn't embrace the introduction of the internet and anticipate its impact on the book industry. The internet introduced a multitude of ways to access and read your sought after text, rather than having to purchase in the old fashioned way of walking into a book store. This, in addition to the impact the internet had on the 'retail' environment as a whole, with the introduction of 'online shopping' and Amazon emerging as a major player, significantly effected many retail book stores. There are many stories like this, where the changing external environment required a major change in how business was done. Choosing to bury your head in the sand, hoping that nothing changes or not acknowledging the need for change, can have serious consequences to any business.

As we've already explored, a human being's need for certainty is a driving factor of their behaviour. This can be detrimental to the success of a business, if the leader is unwilling to embrace and recognise the change required to propel the business forward in the new and ever changing environment. As humans, we will more often than not search for certainty and safety first. When we know what's going to happen, how things will be, then we can feel certain and safe. When change is looming, there's a serious feeling of uncertainty which leads to a feeling of vulnerability and lack of safety or danger. It is a fear of the unknown and because we don't know what lies ahead, we do all we can to stay the same and resist change. This is human nature.

If you are aware of this, and it's a change in your business that is simply 'different' from what you currently know, you can decipher the fear of change as false, because it doesn't pose as any physical threat. Do this by asking yourself, "What specifically am I resisting?" This can help you embrace change to grow and evolve with the business. The reality is that if we don't evolve and change then that's the path we should be most scared of. As the saying goes, we are either green and growing or ripe and rotting. So no change means a slow death, so to speak.

When a change happens, it's easy to jump to conclusions and react in a negative way. The reason for this is because we fast-forward and imagine all the things that could go wrong without knowing all of the facts first. So follow this process to ensure smooth transition in any required change.

1. *Be still, don't react immediately.*

    It's better to say nothing than to react emotionally. Nothing is lost by silently processing information. However, everything can be lost from a big emotional reaction without thinking and processing all of the information.

2. *Seek to understand in detail by asking questions.*

    More than likely, when you become aware of an impending change, you won't have enough information to make an informed decision as to whether or not this is a positive change. Ask as many questions as you need to in order to gain clarity about why, what and how this change is going to happen.

3. *Silence the 'negative voice' that is resisting change.*

    As we explored earlier, the negative voice in your mind comes from the part of your brain known as the amygdala. Its job was to keep us safe from physical danger in prehistoric times when we were under physical threat. This was a handy device in our brain to keep us alive. It certainly ensured our survival.

    In this day and age, in the Western World, it has almost become defunct, as we are not fighting for survival every single day. It therefore perceives any sort of change that is different to what we are currently familiar with as 'danger' or a threat to our physical wellbeing. Therefore, the negative voice inside our mind is fear based and most of the time it isn't a valid fear, it's a perceived fear. By asking ourselves, "What specifically am I fearful of?" and "What will be the consequence? Am I in physical danger?" will help us gain clarity on whether the negative voice is useful and worthy of being listened to in this instance. Usually the answer is, "No, that voice is not worthy or useful."

4. *Look for new perspectives and people who have experienced similar*

    For every different person walking this planet, there is a different perspective for every different situation. So if you don't like your perspective, ask other positive people what their perspective is. How do they know this to be true? Ask them questions about it so you can pick and choose the parts you'd like to adapt to your perspective.

5. *List the benefits of the change*

   From having these conversations, make a list of all the benefits of this change. The more you can find, the more successfully you will adapt to this new change and assist your team to adapt. Pin the benefits up somewhere where the team can see them on a regular basis – maybe in the lunch room – because repetition is key in embracing change.

6. *Seek new knowledge or training if required*

   If you or your team need more 'how' information, then seek out more training to adapt to the new change. If you don't ask, sometimes you don't get.

PURPOSE VS PROCESS

Have you ever worked in an environment where things are done a certain way and nobody actually knows why? Even when you can see that there would be an easier, faster way, people still do it the same way, because that's just how it's always been done. This is one of the most dangerous mindsets a leader and a business can fall into, and it's one of the reasons why Flight Centre is so successful. The company has constantly grown, changed and evolved since its inception in 1983. This is because one of their core philosophies is, "Innovation over conventional wisdom," which means that if someone identifies a better, more productive and functional way of doing something, the company will change it's process to adapt that new approach, rather than sticking with the 'conventional' way, just because that's the way it's always been done.

As leader of your team or business, one of the most important things to embrace as a successful leader is 'change'. If you think of every task as a process that you must complete from step 1 to step 20, then inserting a change at step 8 could seem difficult and maybe even confusing. However, if you think about the purpose – to get to step 20 – all the tasks you perform are simply a vehicle to get you from 1 to 20. Then wouldn't you be keen to change if it meant you found a faster, shorter, more efficient way to get to step 20?

The way to choose the latter is to always remember the reason why you're doing what you're doing. In other words, the purpose of this task. If you know the purpose of why you do what you do, and someone finds a better way to achieve that purpose – which either speeds the process up or makes it easier and less complicated, or creates more success – then why not do that? Relinquish the need to follow the process that we have always known and are familiar with, and embrace the purpose to achieve the best possible outcome.

To remember the 6 Core Human Needs easily, download this complimentary 6 Core Needs poem and questionnaire to help ensure you are meeting all 6 needs of your people. Go to www.leadershipskillsreducethebills.com

PART 5
Focus

Chapter 11:
Ensuring You Have
What You Need

"Inspirational leaders need to have a winning mentality in order to inspire respect. It is hard to trust in the leadership of someone who is half-hearted about their purpose, or only sporadic in their focus or enthusiasm."

~ Sebastian Coe

Now we're moving into the Focus section of the Dynamic Leadership Theorem model and in this chapter we're going to make sure you have everything you need in place to easily direct your focus on a daily basis to obtain the results you are looking for. The thing is, you direct your focus every day already, regardless of whether you're aware of it or not. It's just what you focus on that will determine your results.

Focus is all about how you direct the focus of your team. Unless you give very clear direction to the team about what they must be focussing on, then it's easy for them to become distracted by this shiny thing, or that sparkling thing over there. All of this distraction will lead to a lack in productivity, not because your team intend to waste time, rather because there's no direction for them to push towards.

The first stage to ensuring you're focused is to start with completing the process of implementing your team vision, to ensure your team gains complete buy in and ownership of the vision of the business as well.

We'll also cover:

- Setting your team/business goals.
- Your team's personal goals.
- How to structure for focus.

Once we've looked at how to ensure you and the team have everything in place to focus on what's most important, then we'll move on to exploring some strategies you can implement when things go wrong. And they will.

Completing Your Team Vision

What makes a leader a leader is having people follow them. People don't just follow someone for no reason. There must be a benefit for them to choose to jump on board the leader's bandwagon. For people to follow you as a leader, you must give them a reason to. There must be something attractive for them in the future, a benefit that you talk about, a way that they will feel that will inspire them to jump on your bandwagon. As a leader, where are you going to take your people?

A vision can be described as a guiding image of success. It answers the question, "What does success look like in the future?" It is the idea or picture that unites a team in common effort. It's what the picture looks like once you've achieved: what the company looks like, how the people feel, what people talking about. The statement from Martin Luther King Jr., that began with, " I have a dream," is a perfect example of what a true vision looks and sounds like.

Vision must be communicated with certainty. It's a knowing that things will be different in the future. It can be spoken in metaphor. For example: Martin Luther King, Jr.'s metaphor of "...cashing a cheque, a promise from the architects of the American Republic, a written constitution and declaration of independence, stating a promise that all men, black and white, would be guaranteed the rights of life, liberty and the pursuit of happiness." He then goes on to say that "... America defaulted on this promise." Which was when the "... bank cheque bounced that was given to the Negro people, a failing promise the result, the cheque marked 'insufficient funds'." This is another term that is universal that all people can understand. A good vision also references those who doubt the vision improvement/ change. This unites the team and drives them to take massive action.

Review the vision you've written for your business from the beginning of this book. Given it is still the picture of your success, it's now time to rewrite the story for your team. Begin the story by setting the scene. Build the picture of success. E.g. Where is the picture located, what is happening in the picture and who is there? What has been achieved and how is your team celebrating? Who doubted the achievement and what are they saying now? Then, ask questions (as below) throughout the story, so there are answers required as you read your story to your team. These are the questions your team will answer in their own mind, giving them a greater sense of ownership of this vision as they visualise their answers. Explain to them at the beginning, that you will ask them questions, and they don't need to answer them out loud, simply in their own mind, to avoid and unnecessary interruptions to your story and the mood in the room.

Throughout the story, ask questions like:

- How do you feel?
- What are you noticing now?
- What do you now get to experience because we achieved this vision?

- How is your life easier?
- What does achieving your part of the vision feel like?
- Who is celebrating with you?
- What are people saying to you?
- What are you saying to each other?

It's now time to share it with your team, to get them on board.

Allocate a day where you can work together as a team without interruption, either in a weekly meeting or conference style, and communicate the date with them. Get them excited for what's about to happen. Then at the beginning of the meeting, ask your team to close their eyes, so they can visualise what you're about to read to them. They could do this sitting up, or if they're willing, lay on the ground to be more comfortable. You could choose to have calm music playing in the background. Get creative and do anything that will help create the atmosphere to enable them to visualise the picture you're about to give them. Make sure there isn't loud background noise that could distract them.

It's important that your team have complete buy in to the vision. This story is the framework for your people to contribute to your vision, because the best and easiest way to gain buy-in is get them involved in the process of developing the vision or picture of success. Once you've read them the story of your vision, break the team into pairs and ask them to answer the following questions with short one sentence answers:

Allow no longer than 2 minutes per question.

1. How do you see your team differently by the selected date?
2. What do you believe your individual purpose is in this vision – what value do you contribute?
3. What do you believe the purpose of the team you work in is?

4.   What makes your team unique?

5.   What do you want your legacy to be once you've moved on from your role?

6.   What do you want the future to be for your team?

7.   What does success feel like?

8.   What are people saying to you when you've achieved it?

Then, based on their answers, ask each team to come up with one or two analogies or metaphors for your team and what you want to achieve, like Martin Luther King Jr. did with the 'bounced cheque'. For example: "We are sailors navigating our way to success in rough seas," or, "We are shining stars, brightening the lives of all who we connect with." The benefit of coming up with metaphors is that it gets your people to expand their mind and explore different ways of thinking about what success means to them.

Then come together and have each pair share their answers and metaphors. Ensure that you are facilitating in a way that gives each pair an opportunity to share their ideas and thoughts. Look for areas of agreement and allow the conversation to flow as new ideas emerge. The desired outcome is to find language and imagery that your team can relate to as their vision of success. The analogy or metaphor can be in line with your story or something totally different as a representation of your story and vision.

As a team, select the best analogy or metaphor that represents your team's intention. Your picture is still the foundation to the vision and the metaphor is how it's summarised. If the metaphor or analogy doesn't grab you immediately, don't pursue in a group situation. If you cannot decide as a team in this sitting, then invite one or two people to take the ideas and come up with two or three suggestions of what the vision can be, based on all of the ideas presented, and hold a vote at a later date. The majority wins.

Setting Your Team/Business Goals

Not having any goals is like playing basketball with no hoops, simply running around the court with no aim or goal to shoot for. If you've got nothing to aim for or you're not clear on what direction you want to go, then you just end up pointlessly running around in circles being busy, but not actually achieving anything. If you can imagine, the basketball team would become pretty bored and deflated very quickly without a goal to go for, which would lead to poor morale and negative attitudes. When you have clearly-defined goals, it's very easy to know when you've hit the goal, which means you can celebrate with the team, boosting team morale and inspiring them to keep going.

A goal is the object of a person's ambition or effort; an aim or desired result. There are many different ways for setting goals, but one of the more common and effective ways of setting goals is to follow the S.M.A.R.T formula. It can be easy to misunderstand what goals are and how to set them. To help you avoid some of the common mistakes when setting goals, here are a few examples:

- Set a goal to sell more of a particular item, or to have happier customers, having no reference to what the measurable part of the goal is.
- Set a goal that is out of your control like to serve a certain number of customers per day, or go for something way out of reach that has never been achieved before.
- You may have a goal but don't set a date when it's to be achieved by.

These are all very common mistakes when setting goals. The problem is that when there is no clarity it's very difficult to know when you have achieved what you set out to achieve. The problem with not knowing when you've achieved is that it becomes quite deflating for the team. As I mentioned before, the best part about having a goal is knowing when you've achieved it and then celebrating in style with the team.

So to avoid any of the above mentioned mistakes, follow the S.M.A.R.T model.

S is for Specific. When setting a goal, it's important to ensure that you are setting a very specific goal. Rather than being vague, get very specific about what it is you want to achieve.

M is for Measurable. Avoid being ambiguous and get very clear on the number you'd like to achieve.

A is for Achievable. To know what number you want to achieve, you must also know where you're at now in relation to that number to ensure that it's an achievable goal. This will highlight a clear gap that you need to close.

R is for Realistic. Looking at where you're at now and what you want to achieve, is it realistic? Is it a goal that is going to motivate and inspire your team, or will they be deflated because the goal is unachievable, so they they wonder what the point of trying is.

Finally, **T is for Time-lined**. Set a date of when you want to achieve this by, so you know how long you have to achieve it. The best part about setting a date is that it gives you the opportunity to work backwards. For example: if you are going to achieve X by this date, then you can work out what you need to achieve by each landmark date between now and then, giving you 'stepping stones' to aim for. When you break down goals in this way, it makes it a lot easier to get your head around and doesn't seem like too big a jump to begin with. It also gives you the ability to celebrate smaller successes along the way.

If you're setting yearly goals to achieve for the financial year, it can seem like a lifetime from July to June the following year or from January to December, and it's difficult for people to get their head around seeing that far into the future. Whatever goal you set, with a yearly time-frame, there will be no urgency to take any action now as you've got a whole year to achieve it. So it's important to break down your yearly goals into 90-day goals and then monthly goals, and then possibly even weekly goals. You could even go as far as breaking that down into daily goals if you choose. It just depends on the type of goal that you are going for and if it makes sense to break down into a daily goal, or if keeping it at a monthly goal is enough. This will bring the goal into reality now, and create a sense of urgency to take action.

For example: if you want to achieve a conversion rate of 60% by the end of the financial year and you currently have a conversion rate of 20%, then it seems like quite a big task, and because you have a year to do it in, there's no urgency to take action today.

Create that urgency for your team by breaking it down into bite-size pieces. An even and progressive 90 day goal would be to increase by 10% every 90 days. So you've hit 30% by the end of Quarter 1, 40% by end Quarter 2, and so on. Then each month you would have a goal of increasing your conversion rate by 3.33% which is a third of your 90 day goal. For this type of goal, that's probably as far as you would take it, as a conversion rate is also subject to time. Can you see how it seems much easier to wrap your head around and more achievable to increase your conversion rate by 3.33% per month than to focus on improving your conversion rate by 40% in a year?

The more clarity you and your team have around your goals, the more likely you are to achieve them, because you have a hoop to aim the basketball at to give yourselves the best chance of getting the goal. You can also begin to celebrate the smaller wins, along the way on a monthly or quarterly basis. When you achieve a monthly goal, celebrating that will create more reasons to celebrate, as they say, 'success breeds success'.

Your Teams Personal Goals

A great way to add even more power to your vision and business goals is to relate your team's personal goals to them. Helping someone identify their own personal goals may well be a very unfamiliar conversation to them, as very few people have actually thought about what their goals are in life, let alone written them down.

Interviewers surveyed a group of graduates from the Harvard MBA program in 1979. They found that 84% of graduates had no specific goals, 13% of them had goals but hadn't written them down, and only 3% of them had specific goals written down with clear plans to achieve them.

In 1989, interviewers again interviewed those same graduates and found that the 13% of graduates who had goals were earning twice as much as the 84% who had no goal. Even more staggering is the fact that the 3% who had clearly-defined goals with a plan of action were earning on average ten times more than the entire 97% of graduates combined.

In fact, most people spend more time planning a holiday than they do planning their life. Helping someone establish their personal goals is a privilege and when you do, you will have made a significant impact on the direction of both their career and also their life, in a positive way.

The key to this is to ask them questions. There is no right or wrong here. This is not about knowing the answer. No one knows the answers to these questions better than themselves. They know themselves the best and your opinion on their goals is not relevant. In other words, don't be attached to what their life goals are.

So what's the benefit for you? Imagine you are pushing to achieve a team goal and you say to your team member, "Hey, just achieve these KPI's and that will help us achieve our team goal." Compare that with the leverage you would have if you were to say, "Okay, so in order to move you one step closer to that promotion you've been dreaming about [connected to their goals], you will need to achieve these KPI's, which will give you this result." Presenting their work goal in the context of their personal goal gives you much more leverage and they would have much more ownership on the work goal. This means you will have a self-motivated team rather than a team that requires you to push them every step of the way.

Linking your individual goals to your team's goal is a much more sustainable way of leading and achieving your vision. It takes less energy on your part because they are inspired to achieve their personal goals, and will feel valued as you are supporting them as a person, which will in return give them complete ownership on their work goal. Essentially it is all about working out the WIIFM – 'What's In It For Me?' If you can show them what they are going to get out of their hard work, then you will have a team full of people willing to work hard.

I suggest you look at it this way: "They may be working with us for a week, a year or a decade. However long they are with us, it's my job, as their leader, to ensure that we are helping them move towards their personal goals, regardless of what they are." So, get curious about them as a person and ask them questions to find out what makes them tick.

The most basic model you can use is:

1.   What would you like to achieve in your career in the next 5 years?

2. What do you want to achieve in the long-term, in relation to your finances?

3. What material possessions would you like to *own* in the future?

4. How do you plan on developing and growing as a person with self-awareness?

5. What are your goals in relation to health and fitness?

6. Is there anything else you would like to achieve, personally?

With each of these questions you can drill down by asking them questions like:

- What specifically do you mean by that?
- Tell me more about that.
- What does it look like?
- What does it feel like?

With each goal, remember to apply the S.M.A.R.T. formula.

The better you understand, and therefore *they* understand, what their long-term goals are, the easier it will be to link them to their current role. If you can't find a link, then you can simply ask:

"Okay, so how do you see what you're doing right now linking with that?"

The key to this is the follow up. It's no good having this conversation once and then never mentioning it again. You may as well never have the conversation in the first place.

Have them select one key goal that they would like your help in achieving. Ideally, this is the one that is linked to and drives them to achieve their work goal.

Write the goal at the top of their weekly, monthly or quarterly review template, so you can reference their goal and ask them how they are tracking. Relating the review to their personal goal is also a powerful way to get traction on them achieving what you want them to achieve professionally.

Structure For Focus

As I've mentioned previously, Anthony Robins states that one of the 6 core needs of every human being is that of certainty. Another study of human needs is Maslow's *Hierarchy of Needs Pyramid*. There is much we can learn from this model in relation to leadership, however we'll touch on it only briefly, on a basic level. According to Maslow, the hierarchy of needs is based on where humans will be motivated most. He states that the first need we must fulfil is that of physiological needs: food, water, clothing and shelter. When you have certainty about your immediate environment, you can become motivated and focus on other things.

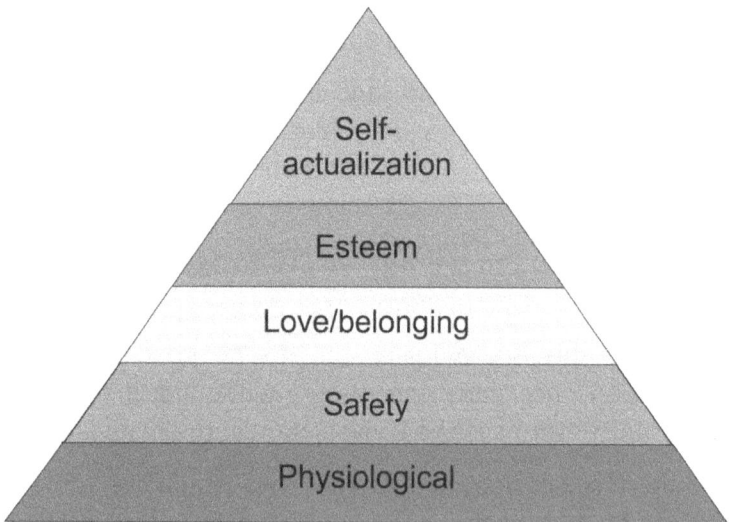

The vast majority of us have certainty about where we will sleep tonight. We know that we have a roof over our head and that it will be a warm and comfortable night's sleep, which frees up our mind to focus on other things.

Now, imagine if you didn't know where you would be sleeping tonight. As a generalisation, homeless people tend to spend their days searching for where they're going to sleep, where they're going to get their next meal from and how they are going to obtain any money they need. Because they haven't got certainty around the basic physiological needs, they have little motivation or capacity to focus on anything else.

On a completely different level, it's similar for people in the workplace. If there is uncertainty about their immediate environment, a lack of safety, uncertainty about their job or what it takes to be successful, then they will not be able to focus on anything other than pure survival. It is for this reason that providing a clearly-structured and safe environment is critical to the certainty and safety of the team members, to allow them to focus on achieving success.

According to dictionary.com, providing a structured environment means "to give a structure, organisation, or arrangement to; construct a systematic framework for". Essentially, this means to establish a routine to ensure that everything that must happen, does happen because it's a part of the weekly or monthly structure that you have established in your business.

The better you build the structure in your business, the more solid your results will be. Think of it in the context of a bridge. If you have a flimsy structure which has pieces missing and breaks at the slightest gust of wind, you're not going to feel very safe, let alone want to use that bridge. But if you are on the Sydney Harbour Bridge, for example, you are going to feel reasonably safe and certain that it's not going to blow over or break away as you are crossing it.

Think about your business in the context of a bridge. Is it more like the first bridge where you have a haphazard approach and sometimes you hold a meeting and sometimes you don't? Or is it like the Sydney Harbour Bridge, where you have a clear, solid structure and your people know exactly what is going to happen with no surprises. When you hold a meeting, is there a clear and communicated agenda? Is it relevant to your people and is it valuable for them to be there? Do they know when to expect these meetings to occur and what topic will be discussed?

Reviews can also be an element of uncertainty for your people, when they happen and how often, let alone what the review will be about. To take as much of the uncertainty out of it as possible, ensure that you nominate the same date each month or quarter to conduct their review and make sure you stick to that date. This gives them a feeling of safety as they know when it will be held, even though there is still the unknown of what will be discussed. There may be other variables in your business that you could build into your daily and weekly structure to ensure your people feel safe, knowing what to expect, so they can focus on being successful.

As we briefly touched on in chapter 8, the best way I've found to implement solid structure into your business is to incorporate the goals and strategies you have set out in your business plan into meetings that you hold on a daily or weekly basis. This ensures that you focus on and talk about the goals and strategies established in your business plan on a weekly basis, rather than it being lost or shoved in a draw, never to be found or talked about again.

Look at your goals and strategies from your Business Plan.

Allocate the goals into a maximum of 4 different categories. Given that your week starts on a Monday, keep Monday free for your business meeting, where you obtain a clear focus for the week. Then allocate your category subjects from Tuesday to Friday.

For Example (for a sales business):

- Lead Generation
- Conversion
- Product knowledge
- $/sale and Referral strategies

On Tuesday, you could look at the strategies you have established for your lead generation goal. What's working, what's not working? Did you achieve your goal for last week? What do you need to do to improve for this week coming? Who was the best performer? Acknowledge and recognise those outstanding performers.

On Wednesday, you could look at your conversion rate for the past week and month. What are your team members doing really well and what are they struggling with? Identify reasons for poor conversion, e.g. not following the sales process or lack of product knowledge. Decide on a plan to improve. Highlight outstanding performers and recognise. Train and retrain one part of the sales process. Ask the performers to explain how they follow the sales process. Give them a heads up if you are going to ask them to do this, so they can have something prepared.

On Thursday, you could up-skill your team in the product knowledge they are missing or require based on conversion rates.

On Friday, you could acknowledge successful members of your team who have achieved the highest average sale value or referral percentage. Ask them what they are doing to achieve this. Have them share how they think about it, what they say, etc. You could train your team on how to increase their average sale value and give them a script to practise and use. As a team you could also brainstorm ways to attract repeat and referral business.

Your Monday morning meeting can be an overview of the whole business. What your results are, what areas need focus and what to address in the upcoming subject meetings – general required communication, like rosters, holidays etc. This meeting can also include any announcements or upcoming changes that need to be communicated. It's like taking a bird's eye view of the business and ensuring that each area of the business, e.g. Sales, Marketing, Finance, Product, etc., is running effectively. It's an opportunity to work on the business, rather than in it with your team.

In each meeting, it is essential that you allow some time for the day's focus. Who's got what on and who needs help? What is the team goal today? etc. This should only take 5-10 min.

To ensure that you are prepared for your meetings, it's also important that you take the time out to prepare and plan all meetings. This doesn't need to take hours, but just give yourself the opportunity to know what your one key message is for that meeting. I usually suggest that you take this time out on a Friday to plan for the upcoming week. If you have a clear structure, this shouldn't take you more than an hour.

Once you know what the daily subjects are for each meeting, you can then prepare a template to follow so that everything that needs to be covered is covered. Then during the meeting, you can allocate one person to be the scribe to take notes, and another is to run the meeting, to keep the conversation flow happening. Once you have this system working in your business, it's a great relief because now you can take a day off or have a holiday and be assured that your people are still gaining the focus required each day.

To provide the highly-supportive environment we've spoken about, depending on the experience level of your team, set a day per week, fortnight or month where you give them an hour of your time for one-on-one focus to address any performance issues and help them improve. If you are disciplined with this, you will find your team will ask fewer questions and they'll feel safe and supported. Because you are providing a high level of support and structure, you may notice a significant improvement to your staff retention, which will have a huge impact on your bottom line as you will save on recruitment and training costs not to mention increased productivity.

ACTIVITY:

Designing Your Structure:

Make a list of all the 'subjects' you must discuss on a weekly basis in your business. Include all the goals you have on your Business Plan and allocate them into four categories. Remember you have your Weekly Business meeting for any staffing/HR discussions. These subjects are specifically around your team's performance.

For example: Customer Service, Lead Generation, Marketing, Sales Performance, just to get you started.

CATEGORY	CATEGORY	CATEGORY	CATEGORY
SUBJECT 1:	SUBJECT 2:	SUBJECT 3:	SUBJECT 4:
_____	_____	_____	_____
_____	_____	_____	_____
_____	_____	_____	_____
_____	_____	_____	_____
_____	_____	_____	_____
_____	_____	_____	_____
_____	_____	_____	_____
_____	_____	_____	_____

Each category is a meeting subject where you discuss any or all of the information in that list.

Look at your week and establish 4 meeting time slots, ideally at the beginning of the day when you can hold meetings each week at the same time. Consider rosters, business hours, external visits, etc.

Select the first day of the week for your 'Weekly Business Meeting'.

Then add in your category subject into the following 4 meeting time slots so your week looks the same regardless of what actual week of the year it is. When you communicate this, it ensures that your team will know what meeting to expect on any given day.

Chapter 12:
What To Do When
S--t Hits The Fan

*"I don't measure a man's success by how high he climbs
but how high he bounces when he hits bottom."*

~ George S. Patton

Regardless of how good a leader you are, there are always times when things go wrong, people lose focus, you lose motivation or the team loses sight of that vision. It's a fact of human nature no one person can remain on and pumped and positive 100% of the time, so to expect to is unrealistic.

So rather than bury your head in the sand, let's take a look at what strategies you have available to you to get back on track when things go wrong. As I've said many times in this book, having the awareness of the problem is often 95% of the solution. So be sure to consciously check on your team morale, the environment and the results regularly, so you can arrest any downward trends before they become out of control.

There are three key strategies I want to share with you that you can implement once you become aware of the problem. They are:

- Refocusing
- What to do when you derail
- How to get out of a rut

Once we've looked at this, we'll be ready to move into the final section of the DLT model, in creating a solid Game Plan.

Refocusing

In the day-to-day operations of running a business it can be easy to get caught up in the craziness of what is happening in the moment. Imagine that you really want a sailing boat. More than anything else, you decide that you absolutely must have a sailing boat. This sailing boat will signify your success and achievement, and propel you ahead in life.

You have fallen in love with it and will do whatever it takes to get it. To ensure you can remain focused on it, you decide you'll take a photo of it and because the boat is in the water, you have to zoom in to get a close up shot of just the boat. So you zoom in and centre the sailing boat in the picture frame. You take the premium shot! The sailing boat is perfectly centred in the middle of the picture, you can see the front of the boat and the back where the captain would sit and the beautiful sails that reach to the sky.

What else do you see in this picture? Maybe a bit of water and some of the sky, but other than that, you can see nothing else. You are now focused on the sailing boat of your desire because you're zoomed in. You remove the camera from your eyes, and now what can you see? Everything else around you. No doubt there is more water, some land, maybe even a mountain off to the side. You can see some buildings and maybe even some cars.

It's easy to lift your head and look around at everything else – and even get preoccupied with the next pretty shiny thing, for example, a car that captures your eye – and so you take a photo of it. As you are looking at the car, what are you not looking at?

That's right, you're not focusing on your sailing boat. You don't see your sailing boat in that picture.

Now relate this back to your business. The sailing boat you took a photo of represents your vision. It is what you decided you wanted to achieve and were committed to working hard to obtain. The car represents everything else that gets in your way and takes your focus, like daily tasks, things you don't like doing but need to, other people's agendas, things going wrong, etc.

If you remain focused on the picture of the car, what are you going to get more of? You're going to get more 'image' of the car, aren't you? The longer you look at it, the more detail you're going to notice about this car. In fact, when you study it for long periods of time, intensely, you are going to become so familiar with it, that you probably won't even need to look at the picture, you'll just be able to visualise it in your mind. So in your business, the more you focus on other things, like the daily tasks, things you don't like doing but have to, other people's agendas and all the things that go wrong, the more familiar you will become with all of these things.

As you are so intently focused on the car, what are you not looking at? You're not looking at or focusing on your sailing boat. The more you look at the car, the less you remember the detail of the boat. So when you relate this back to your vision, it's important that you always remain focused on your vision. Focus on your vision as you complete these tasks and ask yourself if these tasks are going to help you achieve the vision? If the answer's 'yes', great, keep going. If the answer's 'no', then stop and reevaluate why you are doing these tasks.

If for some reason, and it absolutely does happen, you realise that you've been side-tracked, lost your way or even feel like you're not sure why you're doing this, then it means you've lost sight of your vision and you must reset, to focus on what your big picture is.

To refocus means to focus once again. Given that you begin with your vision in mind or what you want to achieve in the business you are working in, then to refocus is to focus once again on your vision – e.g. the boat. Remember, this is your 'big reason why', you get out of bed in the morning, what drives you and inspires you to do your best. Keeping this at the forefront of your mind is crucial to your business success. If you don't have it at the forefront of your mind, and allow all sorts of different things to get in the way – e.g. the car, then where do you think your team is focused? Their focused on the car too, aren't they? The sailing boat has faded into the background and it's now at the back of their mind, as some distant memory of a conversation you had once, never to see that picture again!

As I mentioned, it can be quite easy to get caught up in the day-to-day business and get pulled down in the doldrums of working life. Wow, I make it sound so dreary! So it's important to be aware of where your focus is. The best clue to where your focus is aimed is how you are feeling. If you are feeling weighed down and unmotivated, then you're focusing on the day-to-day busyness and are in 'doing' mode, just trying to tick the boxes. Should you find yourself in this position, then you must stop. Nothing you do in this state will help you achieve, in fact, it will more than likely derail you more.

So to refocus:

1. Acknowledge the feeling of being weighed down and unmotivated (or whatever it is for you) and recognise what you're focusing on.
2. Stop what you're doing, go for a walk, refresh and do something nice for yourself and your team.
3. Reconnect with your vision, your purpose to remember your big reason why.
    a. You can do this by talking about it, adding to your vision, re reading the story of your vision and asking

everyone to bring something to work that represents your vision to them.

4. Acknowledge how you are feeling now that you're refocused.

ACTIVITY:

Re-write these steps and have them close by at work, so if you are feeling a little lacklustre, you can reference these steps and refocus on what drives and inspires you.

What To Do When You Derail

It may be easy to assume that once you're a Leader and you've 'learned' leadership, you may somehow know it all and no longer have any problems! Let me assure you that nothing could be further from the truth. There is always another challenge to deal with or problem to overcome. After all, you are dealing with the greatest uncertainty, people's behaviours.

Regardless of how awesome your environment is or how good a leader you are, there will be times when things go wrong, whether it is miscommunication between your team members, disagreements, frustrations because one person is not pulling their weight or difficulty adapting to change. The causes of friction and unhappiness can be endless. It's a fact of human nature. You cannot prevent this from happening. What you can do is lead in a way that it doesn't extend into something bigger than it needs to be. As the environment is fluid, it can change in any moment, so the way you manage these situations will determine the quality of your environment and your success.

So what does it look like if the team is beginning to derail? There are two types of people to be aware of: those that avoid confrontation, and those that seek it out. If they seek out confrontation, it may start with niggling comments towards each other, which are quite subtle. It can then build into a public and explosive disagreement if left unaddressed. If they don't like confrontation, they will most likely complain to you in a one-on-one situation, asking you to deal with it.

How you handle this is crucial to the quality of your environment. Like I've said before, you must protect your environment like it is your mother. You must protect your environment because your success, and more importantly, your reputation depends on it. If you are also one to avoid confrontation, the danger is that you discard the situation, put your head in the sand and do nothing. The problem with this is if you do this repeatedly, not only will your team begin to lose respect for you as a leader, the situation will eventually bubble to the surface and it will be much worse than dealing with the original problem.

Alternatively, if you over-handle the situation, you will be seen as a leader who micro-manages and loves drama, someone who gets involved in everyone's petty little issues and makes things worse than what they originally were. Handling any issue in this way will also lead to your team losing respect for you and will make the situation much worse than it needs to be. So it's important that you understand how to handle the situation 'just right', not too little or too much, just right.

Let's look at how to handle the one-on-one conversation first, where a team member has confided in you expressing their frustration with a fellow team member. It's important for you to understand that, even though you're the leader, it doesn't mean they get to dump the problem on you and then they don't have to think about it anymore. It is not your problem to deal with, and you must teach them that.

At the beginning of this book, we talked about Responsibility. As their leader, it is your job to teach them about their ability to take responsibility for themselves and their experiences. There is a series of questions you can ask to help them learn how to deal with the situation. You do not, I repeat, you do *not* have to deal with the situation for them. That would be like doing homework for a teenager, and they will not learn if they don't do it themselves.

This is called 'rescuing' and you do more harm than good if you rescue people.

A great example of rescuing comes from a farmer and his son. As they were out in the paddock they saw a cocoon. The butterfly inside the cocoon seemed to be squirming and struggling to get out. The little boy exclaimed, "Dad, Dad, the poor butterfly is struggling, we need to help it!" So they went up to the house and got a tiny pair of nail scissors. The farmer ever so carefully edged the scissors into the cocoon and cut it away to allow the butterfly to emerge with ease. But when it was released, it couldn't fly. It fell to the ground and died. The son was devastated by this, and what they didn't realise is the very act of the struggle for the butterfly is what pushes all the fluid down to the end of its wings, giving it the ability to fly. Because it didn't have that full struggle opportunity, its wings didn't develop and it was unable to fly.

Your job as their leader is not to rescue them from discomfort, but to teach them to become a better version of themselves and push through the struggle. When you do, that's when they will be able to fly. So, here are the questions:

1. What is the current reality of the situation?
2. Let them go for a minute and then help them by asking them only to talk in facts. You're not interested in any 'he said, she said' scenarios. What are the actual facts of the situation?
3. How would they like the situation to be/what is their desired outcome?

4. What possibilities exist to be able to rectify the situation? Help them to brainstorm all the possible options.

5. Which possibility would they like to choose to take action on?

6. Do they feel they can have this conversation with the individual concerned themselves? Encourage them to have the conversation themselves because if they want you there, there's another whole dynamic you need to deal with before you go about doing that.

7. Give them a step-by-step plan of how to approach it. The key to this step is to have them start the conversation with, "When this happens, I feel..." or, "I feel... when you do this."

By using 'I feel' statements, no one can tell them they are wrong, because it's how they feel. This removes any need for people to become defensive or feel attacked. When you follow this process you are helping them to own their feelings and frustrations. They don't get to use you as a dumping ground. They must take responsibility for it and then take action to rectify it.

It's important for them to know that you support them and believe that they can have this conversation successfully. The thing is, they won't want to do it beforehand, but once they walk away having done it, they will feel on top of the world. This is a much better outcome than if you rescued them and did it for them. You've taught them not only how to take responsibility and address their own problems, but also that they can't just dump their problems on you and expect you to deal with them. You'll notice a reduction in the number of issues you have to deal with if you handle situations this way.

It is very similar if you are dealing with a team situation. If it's more than just one person who has the problem, then you can hold a team meeting. Be careful that it's not a 'gang up on one person' session. If all the problems are to do with one person only, then it must be dealt with one-on-one. You would follow the above process and then potentially back it up with a conversation with the individual yourself to manage their response and help them see through to an action plan of how to improve.

If there are a number of issues that people have with a number of different people, then follow the process below. Prior to the meeting have a brief one-on-one conversation with each team member to advise them that you will be holding a team meeting and it's essential that each person is there.

If one person can't be there, then you MUST choose a different time to hold the meeting where everyone can be there. To begin the meeting, explain to them that they must only speak with statements beginning with "I feel..." so it's a calm and non-attacking conversation.

1. You facilitate the meeting by stating the situation as you understand it or invite someone to begin by doing the same.

2. You ask each person to express how they feel about the situation using 'I feel' statements.

3. Ensure that you follow up each person's statement with a question on how they would like it to be, so every person articulates how they see the problem being resolved and each individual on the receiving end knows how to change their behaviour.

4. Have each team member articulate what they will change as a result of this conversation in 1 or 2 sentences to ensure understanding.

5. Agree on changes and state the overall outcome for the team.

There is a great saying that 'Success isn't about getting rid of all of your problems, rather learning who you need to be to deal with and over come them.' When you learn how to manage conflict within your team and help them refocus on what is important, then you can be certain that your environment will go from strength to strength.

Getting Out Of A Rut

As we discussed in the last section, no matter how good a leader you are and how good your environment is, it is still possible to fall into a rut. This can happen for a number of reasons and can happen to either just one individual or the whole team. Maybe you've had to deal with a number of difficult customers in a row or the pile of work seems to be growing and you don't seem to be reaping any reward. The cause of the rut is irrelevant. That fact is, you can slip into a negative mindset easily and it doesn't feel good, give you good results or make you, or anyone else for that matter, happy. In fact, the longer you leave it unaddressed, the worse it will get. Not acknowledging a rut for either yourself or your team can have severe consequences and can cause irreparable damage to your environment.

Previously, we talked about focus and how what you focus on is what you get and you exclude everything else. When you're in a rut, you're focusing on what is wrong, what isn't working and how difficult everything is. You typically use words that overgeneralise that one thing means everything. This means you are feeling negative emotions, like helplessness, apathy, defeat. This is the being part of the "Be/Do/Have" model. When you feel these emotions, it leads to uninspired, unmotivated and negative actions, which gives you poor or negative results.

The official definition of a rut is "a habit or pattern of behaviour that has become dull and unproductive, but is hard to change". I'd like to change just one thing in this definition, and that is alter the final part to, 'it's unfamiliar to change.' 'Hard' as a word has a horrible, almost impossible, energy about it, whereas 'unfamiliar' is lighter and makes it sound more possible to make a change, you've just got to figure out how.

So let's take a look at how to get out of a rut:

1. Acknowledge the situation and take responsibility.

    The first step towards getting you or your team out of a rut is to acknowledge it. As I've mentioned before, Awareness is 95% of the solution to the challenge. When you are aware that you're in a rut, then and only then can you do something about it. While this sounds pretty simple, it can be difficult because, ultimately, it requires you to take responsibility for where you're at. Your feelings are the best clue to becoming aware of being in a rut. If you are having negative feelings, feeling down, what's the point, I can't be bothered – they are all clues that you are in a rut and you need to stop and take some time to address the issues.

    It's even more important to acknowledge if one of your team members has fallen into a rut because most people aren't aware when they begin to fall into the negative mindset. This takes some practice as it's about taking notice of your people and what they are not saying. The best clue for you will be in their body language, their tonality and the words they are using. Their body language will typically be closed – shrugged shoulders, slouched spine and low energy. Their tonality will be low, possibly even monotonous and uninspired, and the words they use may be blasé and negative. You may notice just one aspect of their communication that has fallen, however the moment you recognise it is the time to jump on them. (Not literally.)

2. Chunk down.

    Now that you're aware of being in the 'rut', you need to figure out exactly what has caused it. When you find yourself or a team member in a rut, typically they will be looking at and processing the information in larger chunks unable to identify what the problem is. So it's important that you chunk down and get to the nitty gritty of what the problem is. So you need to ask yourself or your team member the question, "What specifically is the problem?"

    You can help them by breaking their role or the business into different sections and get them to rate it out of 10, with 10 being feel really positive about it and 1 being feel really negative about it. The different sections could be, for example, Sales, Marketing, Finances, Customers, Admin. Once they have rated each one of them out of ten, then you can zero in on the problem areas. You may find that there are multiple problems, so with each section of the business or their role that is rated at a 6 or less, you will need to address. Then explore that section by asking, "Tell me about (area rated under 6)?"

    Listen to their language for where the problem is. Be careful not to give them the answers when doing this, as they will not have the breakthrough they need. If you are in the rut, then you must write this down or ask your 2IC to ask you these questions. Then chunk them down by asking, "So what specifically is the problem with (area rated under 6)?" Keep asking this question until you get to the specific issue, then you can help them work out steps to climb out of the rut.

3. Language creates reality.

What you focus on is what you get, and there's another step. What you focus on is also what you talk about and what you talk about is what you get! For example: you don't hear a poor person talking about their shopping excursions and how much fun they had spending hundreds of dollars, do you? And typically you wouldn't hear a wealthy person talk about how they never buy anything because they can't afford it either. So once you've got to the bottom of what the problem is, you must ask them how they want it to be, and get them to articulate how they want that situation to be in positive 'towards' language.

4. Quality of your questions – Why vs How.

    World class coach and motivational speaker Anthony Robins states in his book *Awaken the Giant Within* that the quality of the questions you ask yourself will determine the quality of your experience. Think about when you are asked a question starting with 'why'. For example: "Why did you do that?" or "Why didn't you do it this way?" What is your immediate response? You want to jump to defend yourself, don't you, giving you no time to think about a new way of thinking. You are simply defending what you did, even if you know you made a mistake. Now think about how you would respond if you were asked a 'how' question instead. "How did you do that?" or "How did you decide to come to that decision?"

Now combine step 3 with step 4, and have them ask themselves "How can I...?" followed by what it is they actually want to achieve or what they want the situation to be like. Notice the energy difference when you say to yourself "Why can't I...?" compared to, " How can I...?".

The important thing to note here, is that you don't need to come up with an answer for this question. In fact, if you do, then you will cut off any other possible solution or outcome that you hadn't thought of yet. This is because the simple act of asking the question means that your focus will be in the right direction to filter in new information. You will feel more empowering emotions which will lead you or them to taking more empowering actions, which will give you a more positive result. For the question to exist, so must the answer, you just have to be patient and wait for it to appear, whilst you maintain the right focus.

So the equation is:

How you feel will determine where you're focused.

↓

Where you're focused will determine the actions you take.

↓

The actions you take will determine what outcome you get.

↓

The outcome you get is what you talk about.

↓

The quality of the question you ask yourself internally, 'Why' vs 'How' will determine your emotions and how you feel and where you're focused.

And so on in an everlasting cycle.

To access your complimentary template of 'How To Design An Effective Morning Meeting/Training' go to www.leadershipskillsreducethebills.com

PART 6
Game Plan

Chapter 13: Bringing It All Together

*"If everyone is moving forward together,
then success takes care of itself."*

~ Henry Ford

Your final step in this six-step system is to bring it all together with your Game Plan. A plan is a clearly identified set of strategies to achieve a specified goal. Often in business, this is only identified in the leader's mind.

Unfortunately, this doesn't help the leader, the staff or the business, because there is little clarity about what must be achieved. It results in the leader becoming stressed and possibly overwhelmed, as they're trying to remember everything all of the time, ultimately not being effective at all. It also doesn't help the staff as they become frustrated because it hasn't been clearly communicated, so they feel like they have to be a mind reader, to know what to focus on and put into action.

Because the leader and the staff are not operating at an optimal level, the business certainly won't be either. All of this can be avoided simply by ensuring that you have a clearly-defined set of strategies that are documented for all to see. So in this chapter we'll be keeping it simple and looking at:

- Your strategies and taking action.

- Your business plan – keeping it simple.

Once we've looked at ensuring your strategies are clearly communicated, we'll move into the final section of ensuring you're working on your business with forethought and proactive thinking, rather than reactive behaviour.

Strategies, Taking Action

Another word for strategies is the 'actions' that you will take and strategies counterbalance the vision in your business plan. The vision is the abstract, the big picture, and is the reason why you work hard and focus each day. Your strategies are the 'how' you will achieve and the specific action steps that you will take that will get you to the vision. Essentially, you could see strategies as the map of how to get to your vision. Needless to say, they are essential to achieve success in your business.

Given that you have now set the vision and goals for your business, it's time to derive the strategies from the goals to achieve them. For each goal that you have on your business plan, you should have 3 strategies to achieve that goal. Why 3, you ask? To keep your business plan simple. You need to have more than 1 to allow for a strategy not to work. Any more than three, and you'll lose focus on any of them and it will become too overwhelming. For example: let's say you have a goal on your business plan to achieve a certain $/customer. Remember, your goal needs to be specific. It also helps to know what the number is now, so you can see the improvement, as we discussed in the goal-setting section.

Do this with your team, hold a brainstorming session. Give them the 'goal' from your business plan and ask them to come up with ideas on how to achieve this goal. Doing this will give them total 'buy in' to the strategies which is essential as they are the ones who will be taking the action.

You could do a simple 'green light' thinking strategy, where you give them the goal and then they have 2 minutes to write down as many possible ways (strategies) they can think of to achieve that goal. Then each person shares theirs and, as a team, you decide on the three most impactful and achievable strategies.

Here is an example of possible strategies to achieve your goal of achieving $xx/per customer:

With every sale:

- Offer a standard insurance or warranty to protect what the customer is purchasing.
- Offer an upgrade of the product they are purchasing.
- Offer a complimentary product when they purchase the upgrade, to improve their experience of the original product.

In the example, each of the strategies have specific actions to take. So the team knows exactly what they must do. When you have clear strategies, there is clarity around what your team members must do to contribute to the achievement of the goal and vision. When you communicate this in such a way that it relates directly to the vision (and they have complete buy in to the vision), then it becomes all the more important for your team to do it, rather than it being just another 'have to'.

Sometimes you may need to break the goal down to a quarterly or monthly goal. This could help you recognise new and different strategies to achieve the goal that weren't immediately obvious when looking at the yearly goal. For example: If you wanted to improve your conversion rate over the year by 40%, you may find this completely overwhelming and not know where to start. Yet, if you were to break it down to a quarterly goal of 10% and a monthly goal of 3.33% increase, it may appear more manageable and ideas to improve may come to you more easily.

Your Business Plan

As we've explored before, imagine getting into your car to go somewhere you've never been before without your phone or a satellite navigation system. Where would you drive? How would you know where to turn? How would you know to make a change to your direction? How would you know if you were on track or not? If you don't have a map, phone or satellite navigation, the chances of you actually finding your destination are minuscule, and if you did actually find it, it would be by accident. This is what you're doing if you run a business without a business plan. If you're not following a plan with specific actions then the chances of you achieving your vision are also minuscule and any success would only happen by accident. We want you to have success on purpose, so that's the reason why you need to have a fluid working plan to follow.

Like I've mentioned before, your business plan is like the road map to your destination or your vision. It's the plan of how you're going to get there. At its most basic, your business plan is made up of your vision, goals and strategies. An important part of achieving your vision is to break down your goals and strategies into 90-day blocks. If you focus on a goal that is meant to be achieved 12 months from now, it can seem quite daunting and overwhelming. So break down your goals to progressive 90-day blocks. This means the 'chunks' of achievement are smaller and guides you to know when you can celebrate progress throughout the year. From here, you can then break down the goals to monthly and then weekly if you so choose. The choice is yours.

Essentially, if you have completed the activities throughout this book, then you have already completed your business plan. Now all you need to do is collate your vision, your goals and your strategies onto one A4 page. To ensure your business plan is a functional and working document, it must fit on one page.

Make sure you have it up around the office so that you and your people can see it, but not necessarily your customers.

Another way to ensure that you are using your business plan as a usable and fluid document is to integrate it with your business meeting. Create a business meeting template where the heading of the meeting is 'your vision'. Then you can have the typical meeting minute details like date, attendees, apologies, etc. Then because your business meeting should be all about achieving your goals and working on the business, the best way to do this is break the meeting down into the different goals you have from your business plan and then sub-points under each goal for the strategies identified from your business plan. This gives you an opportunity each week to look at your strategies, what's working, what's not, what needs attention and how to improve, as well as celebrate what is working and what's on track. Make sure you have someone recording what you discuss each week. A scribe, to record where you're at now and actions you will take to improve. This means you have the ability to follow up easily, look at the progress you've made and ensure that what you've agreed to take action on is actually happening. It's also an example of what and where your focus is, which is a great way to maintain awareness.

If you do this, it means that you are reviewing your business plan weekly and keeping it fresh and up to date, which then means that the time you spent working on it was time well spent, as well as giving you the greatest opportunity to achieve the vision. If you need some assistance with creating your business meeting template, go to www.leadershipskillsreducethebills. com to access the membership area. Here's an example of what a business meeting template might look like:

WEEKLY BUSINESS MEETING
YOUR VISION

To Bring to the WBM:
Documents/Reports Required to know where your business is currently

Date: _____

Attendees: _____

Previous weeks performance

Name:	KPI #1	KPI #2	KPI #3	KPI #4	KPI #5	KPI #6

Overall Performance….. Current and Future

Name	Current Month	Future Month

Sales and Service - Goal/s

What was our focus last week?

What did we achieve?

Insert your goals from your Business Plan

What is our greatest opportunity?

Based on our results what is our Team Focus for this week?

Finance - Goal/s

What was our focus last week?

What did we achieve?

What is our greatest opportunity?

Based on our results what is our Team Focus for this week?

Marketing & Advertising - Goal/s

What was our focus last week?

What did we achieve?

What is our greatest opportunity?

Based on our results what is our Team Focus for this week?

Product - Goal/s

What was our focus last week?

What did we achieve?

What is our greatest opportunity?

Based on our results what is our Team Focus for this week?

People & Communication:

Team Activity

Roster

Meetings

Trainings

Information Sharing:

To download your complimentary copy of this 'Weekly Business Meeting' Template and as an added bonus your very own 'Self Weekly Accountability' Questionnaire to help you stay on track, go to www.leadershipskillsreducethebills.com

Chapter 14: Working On The Numbers

"Follow effective action with quiet reflection. From the quiet reflection will come even more effective action."

~ Peter Drucker

Given that we are at the end of the six-step process to becoming a motivational leader, it's now time to share possibly one of the greatest secrets in business. Don't be fooled by its simplicity, as it is what all successful people do in one form or another. Reflective thinking – taking time out to reflect on your business and assess what's working and what's not. When you combine it with the knowledge you obtain from your KPI analysis, you will begin to learn how to identify future problems and downturns, and will have the opportunity to arrest the problem before it impacts your business significantly on the bottom line. At minimum, you'll be able to reduce the impact. Whilst this appears simple, it's probably the area most leaders find the most challenging. However, if you choose to make it a priority, the time you invest in reflection will repay you in the long-term.

Not A Boring KPI Analysis

When you bake a cake, there is a certain formula that helps produce the desired outcome. There are certain numbers that you follow to add in the right amount of each ingredient, ensuring you obtain the right consistency and taste, resulting in a yummy cake. What would happen if you reduced the amount of flour you added and increased the amount of milk? It would turn into cake soup, and would most likely result in a very flat cake, if it were to resemble a cake at all.

Being a leader requires you to have sound knowledge about the daily, weekly and monthly numbers in your business, ensuring you achieve those numbers to provide consistency in your results. These numbers are also known as the Key Performance Indicators and are the measures of the right amount of each ingredient required to produce your desired outcome.

The right amount of 'new customers', the right amount of 'conversion' from enquiry to customer, the right amount of $/sale to achieve the right level of total sales are all required ingredients of most businesses – just to name a few. Each number will impact the overall result of your business. As a leader, you must know these numbers, because that will give you the understanding of how to ensure your business results rise, as does a successful cake.

Whilst it may seem that knowing your numbers isn't necessarily 'soft skills' of leadership, it is essential to touch on it to ensure you know where your business is at now so that you know what you need to focus on to improve. As a leader of your business, you absolutely need to understand the Key Performance Indicators so you can recognise what's working and what isn't, and make the necessary changes. It's also important that you know how to help your people improve, and if you can't analyse the numbers of your business then you won't have the ability to support them to achieve their goals. So, knowing, understanding and analysing your KPI's leads back to the support of your people to gain ultimate success in your business.

Your KPI's or Key Performance Indicators are just that: they are the key numbers that tell you how well your business is doing. They can vary, depending on what business you are in, however can include things like, number of enquiries; average conversion rate; average $/sale; repeat customer %; etc. As a leader, you should already be aware of what the key indicators are in your business.

Successfully executing your Game Plan requires you to know where your business is at now so you can identify new opportunities to improve. If you are utilising your new 'Weekly business meeting' template from your business plan, then you'll have full knowledge about where your business is at. The great thing about that is you will come to know clearly what your average numbers are, and will be able to arrest any unusual down turns as they happen immediately, rather than be surprised at the end of the month or quarter, having no knowledge of it at all.

Working On Your Business, Not In It

If you continue to drive your car, over and over again, day after day, month after month, year after year and do nothing else, no servicing, no new tyres, no oil change, no cleaning, what would happen to the car? It would deteriorate, wouldn't it? In fact, the longer you neglected it, just getting in and driving, the worse the condition of the car would be. So what do you have to do to maintain the condition of your car? It must be serviced regularly, with new tyres, wheel alignment, new oil and spark plugs, and maybe even wash it every now and again. Essentially, you need to work on the car to maintain its functionality, condition and effectiveness, otherwise you just end up running it into the ground.

It's exactly the same with your business. If you just work in your business, day after day, month after month, year after year, and never take any time out to work *on* the business, then what you are doing is running it into the ground. You must work on your business to ensure its functionality, condition and effectiveness.

Ok, so what does 'working on your business' actually mean? Well, it means taking a bird's eye view of your business or taking one aspect of your business and analysing it thoroughly, searching for ways to improve it. It requires the leader to take on a different perspective, which requires thought and reflection as well as the time to think proactively about the business and how to improve it, rather than always reacting and putting out spot fires.

There are many ways to do this. Some leaders do this naturally and others must make a concerted effort to make the time. If you're someone who is constantly very busy and fill every moment of every day with appointments and activities, then here is one way to begin working on your business, rather than just in it. If you choose to do it, you will be rewarded ten-fold.

Remove yourself from your typical working environment to work on your business. This could be in a quiet room, in a park or in a café – somewhere that you can focus on your thoughts and not be distracted by people, phones or customers and anything else that may take your focus. A great way to do this is to make an appointment in your calendar/diary for the time you plan on doing this for the length of time you require. Then all you need to do is keep that appointment. Make sure you stick to it. The following questions are designed to get you thinking about your business in a way that evokes ideas and inspirations. You should also take time out to plan your next week's business meeting. Whilst you might look at and answer a number of the questions on this list, be sure to introduce only 1 idea at a time to your team. Too much at once will result in nothing being achieved. Select from one of the 14 questions below and answer thoroughly.

1. Look at your Business Meeting template. What part of it indicates you are in automatic mode? How can you refocus and reinspire your team. A change is as good as a holiday.

2. Find one 'number' in your business you need to learn more about and improve, e.g. conversion rates, trial/ sales rates, enquiry rate, average $/sale. Then spend time learning more and then teach your team in a meeting, exploring possible ways to improve.

3. What's one thing you could do that might increase conversion rates by 1%? Just a single additional percent can result in a massive boost in revenue.

4. Identify 3 pieces of evidence about why your latest customers decided to give you money.

5. Identify 3 pieces of evidence about why people didn't buy. The answer to more revenue lies with the customers who didn't buy.

6. Decide on one thing you could do to demonstrate that you're an expert in your field.

7. Identify something of value you could give your customers for free. Maybe a discount on a relevant product, a free book, or an article of interest. Give them something for free to show you care and they'll reward you ten-fold.

8. Do one thing to increase your business visibility on Instagram, Twitter, Facebook, or even write a blog.

9. Come up with an idea to invest in your customers' experience after the sale.

10. Identify one action you can take to become more visible in communities that relate in some way to your business.

11. Identify what sets your business apart from your competitors.

12. Search for the great aspects of the business. Decide on a way to celebrate with your team

13. Establish a new way for your team to collect relevant feedback from your customers and then use the information productively.

14. Survey your existing customers and ask them why they are your customers

Once you have chosen your question – take some time yourself to brainstorm your answers and come up with a plan or an idea. You could also present this question to your team in the weekly business meeting to give them the opportunity also to work on the business. As they say, two heads are better than one. Whichever way you choose to work on your business be sure that you remain on purpose and it is in line with your vision. When presenting it to your team, ALWAYS relate it back to your vision as the reason WHY you are working on this!

You now know the six steps to reducing staff turnover and increasing productivity.

If you want more information around any of the templates or concepts I've discussed in this book go to www. leadershipskillsreducethebills.com for more information and free resources.

I wish you all the best in your leadership journey. Please email me with any questions you may have and I'd love to hear all of your success stories as a result of taking action. Also, for further information about training, you may contact me directly at lisa@motivationalleadership.com.au.

Conclusion

As we've discovered throughout this book, there is a simple process – a system to follow – that will give you all the tools and skills required to be a motivational leader. You now know how to adopt a powerful mindset and believe in yourself and your team. You now have access to some incredible communication tools, giving you the ability to manage any situation. You can now choose to adopt the personal discipline required to be a motivational leader. You now know what a great environment is, but more importantly, how to create one. You're extremely clear on where you must focus and also how to execute your game plan. If you have applied what we have unleashed in the pages of this book, you now know the secret recipe to achieving success.

I believe the best part about being a leader is that leadership is a true reflection of yourself. It will highlight your strengths, as well as your opportunities for self-improvement. When you acknowledge that an issue in your team is a potential reflection of a part of you, and begin to focus on that aspect of yourself, then you will find that the problem in your team will disappear. I know this may be an unfamiliar concept, and certainly even the best leaders have trouble swallowing this from time to time, however, I ask you, "What level do you want to play? A half assed game, or a full game?" When you play the full game, and only when you play the full game and take 'complete' responsibility and ownership for everything that happens in your life and business, then you will realise TRUE success.

Leadership is a journey of self-discovery where you have the privilege to be a part of, have influence over and impact the lives of your team. This is why I value the role so intently. Yes, I love to have fun, however, I know as a leader I am responsible for my team's happiness at work, and their career destiny. What I do and the decisions I make will impact their happiness, both at work and at home.

That's a big responsibility, and I love it.

There is no room for me to prove that I'm right and look like I never make a mistake. I am a human being and very far from being perfect. The examples in this book are just a few of the many mistakes I have made as a leader. I choose to see each mistake as an opportunity to learn, so I don't have to repeat it again. If I learn from it, that's all I, and anyone else, can expect from me.

So choose to let go of the need to be right. Give yourself permission to make mistakes. People are not inspired by a leader who has a need to be seen as perfect. They are inspired by a leader who has worked through adversity and come out the other side with a brighter, more empowered attitude. They are inspired by a leader who has desire to help others achieve. They are inspired by a leader who believes in their people and will do what it takes to help them be successful.

If you focus your energy on and love the people, then the success and money will come. We have spoken a lot about how to make your people happy and helping your people become successful. When you do this, you will achieve all that you desire. As a person who significantly influenced my career once said, "Given we help enough people get what they want, our needs will most certainly be taken care of." If you take care of your people, your people will take care of your customers, your customers will then take care of the business and the business will take care of you and your income.

Another important note I want to leave with you is never, ever give up. The best two qualities you can adopt in leadership and business are perseverance and determination. With these two qualities, you can achieve ANYTHING!! In fact, this is not just in leadership, this is life. There is a huge correlation between the lessons in leadership and lessons in life. What you learn in leadership you can apply in life, and vice versa.

Leadership can be a tough gig, and some days will suck. One of the best pieces of advice I was ever given was "Don't quit on a bad day. If you still don't enjoy what you are doing when you're having a 'good' day, then you are in a position to make the decision." This advice pushed me through many difficult moments, especially earlier in my career. There were many times where I wanted to just throw it all in and do something else. I'm so grateful that I took this advice, because it is the very reason I'm able to share this book with you, and I'm eternally grateful to the very special person who shared it with me – my dad.

If you're committed to being the best version of you that you can be, your leadership skills will reflect that and will continue to improve. There is always another level, something else to learn. As I've mentioned, we are either green and growing or ripe and rotting, so enjoy the process of learning and becoming. The best investment you can ever make is one that you make in yourself. There's lots of success waiting for you, you just need to decide that you're going to take it. As you continue to make the distinctions between good leadership and great leadership, you will be a force to be reckoned with. I wish you all the success and happiness in your leadership journey!

.

Resources

Here are some of the resources that have led to the creation of this book.

- *Awaken The Giant Within'* – Anthony Robbins
- *The Secret* – Rhonda Byrne
- *Ted Talk* – Simon Sinek
- *Maslow's Hierarchy of Needs.* Web. 1 May 2015.
- Myers, David G. "Chapter 12: Motivation and Work." *Psychology.* 7th ed. New York: Worth, 2004
- Diploma of Life Coaching, The Coaching Institute

Acknowledgments

There are many people I would like to thank for assisting me in the creation of this book.

Firstly, I'd like to thank my parents, Mary and Anders Wiking. From the very beginning of my career – in fact, my life – they provided unwavering support and belief in me and my ability. Without your support, especially in the early years of my career, this book would never have been possible. I love you with all my heart. Thanks, Mum and Dad.

Thank you to my dear sister Emma. Without you I also wouldn't be the person I am today. You've taught me love and compassion for all people and it's certainly a quality I take into my leadership environment. Thank you.

I am eternally grateful to Alison Crabb for giving me the opportunity to become a leader all those years ago. You believed in me and gave me the benefit of the doubt when I had nothing but sheer determination. And again, 14 years later, sought me out and offered me my 'dream job'. It was my life ambition to be an area leader and for that opportunity and all the others, I'm forever grateful, Al. Thank you.

To Sharon Pearson. You handed me your business. Trusted me with your most precious possession. You pushed me, guided me, encouraged me and taught me what it took to run a multi-million dollar business. We had an amazing time together, one that I will never forget. I am forever grateful to you for the time you invested in me.

To my very first team, Mark, Peter, Mary-Jo, Stephanie, Jo and Emily – and we did it blindly together. Thank you for having faith in me, for trusting that we could do it, and we did!

To the team of the business we opened from scratch. Callum, Bridie, George and Natalie. You guys helped me believe that what I'd learned was replicable. Callum Brown you're one in a million. Your leadership skills blow me away and I'm forever in awe of the success that you're still continuing to create.

Thank you to my dear friends Michelle Martello, Nicci Latchford, Shanelle Cooper and Elizabeth Tyrell. You have been my rocks through thick and thin, and I've learned so much about life and leadership from you. I love you all to bits.

Emily Gowor, for pushing me to get this book finished. Thank you for being the inspirational soul you are. You'll forever be remembered as a significant influence in my career.

Thank you to Ali Crabb, Graham (Skroo) Turner, Carole Cooper, Marcelle Kurth, Ben Cooper and Stephanie McClounan for agreeing to read the manuscript and offering feedback and suggestions.

To my readers, especially my first two, Cath and Bruce, thank you for trusting me, to provide you with the step-by-step knowledge to becoming a motivational leader. I trust you've found the information I've shared with you valuable. I hope to be able to continue to support you in your leadership development.

Last, but certainly not least, thank you to my beautiful partner in life, Darren Feltus, our gorgeous daughter, Kiara, and our unborn son. Darren, without your love, support and encouragement, this book wouldn't be in existence. Kiara, thank-you for being such a good little girl and great sleeper. You allowed me the time to complete this book. To my little boy, you're already beginning to teach me the next round of lessons that I need to learn. I love you all from the bottom of my heart and feel like I'm the richest person with you in my world.

About The Author

Lisa Wiking is a leadership expert, speaker and published author. Through spending the past eighteen years researching leadership and applying her extensive experience in her own career as a leader, Lisa has established a clear system for what does and does not work in empowering people to rise up as leaders. Along the way, she continues to add new skills to her tool kit.

Having studied a Diploma In Life Coaching, Lisa is a Master Practitioner of Neuro-Linguistic Programming and has completed multiple trainings in public speaking and presenting. Lisa has also led many teams to success – teams as small as 4 or 5 members to teams of over 100 people. Complimented by her supreme training and public speaking skills, Lisa captivates audiences – both small and large – and engages them in a way that ensures leadership improvement in any organization.

Lisa offers Motivational Leadership's flagship training Dynamic Leadership Theorem through a series of e-course trainings to enable the leader to work at their own pace, implementing throughout the course. They also get to experience the support of the online 'DLT' Community for life. On completion, the participants find themselves being the Motivational Leader.

Lisa is absolutely passionate about assisting leaders to experience leadership as it should be: an empowering and rewarding experience. Lisa is committed to helping leaders across the globe provide happy and empowering workplaces, spreading a little more happiness throughout the world.

Are you ready to increase your profits and reduce your bills?

Work with Lisa to implement the concepts of *Dynamic Leadership Theorem* into your business in greater detail via her comprehensive, self-paced e-course!

During this 8 Week e-course – complete with downloadable worksheets, DVDs and PowerPoint slides – Lisa will take you on a journey to gain a deeper level of understanding of leadership and apply the learning into your organization as you participate in the training. This course gives you a profound opportunity to achieve your desired results of reducing staff turnover and increasing productivity.

Participating in this 8 Week course will give you a life time membership to the online private Facebook group, giving you the chance to connect with a growing community of like minded leaders. You will have the chance to share your successes, gain help and support with your challenges, share and gain new ideas and thoughts about how to be a motivational leader.

You will also gain free access to the membership resource centre, offering you all of the templates and scripts mentioned in this book, along with many other valuable documents, giving you a library of resources at your fingertips, ready to offer the solution to your next leadership challenge (valued at $97 per annum).

One of the best investments you can ever make is the investment in yourself. The knowledge will remain with you forever and repay you tenfold.

For full details on the above training and other training opportunities, go to: www.leadershipskillsreducethebills.com